I0015787

Software Engineering as a Career: How to Land a Programming Job without a Computer Science Degree, Habits of Successful Self-Taught Coders and Avoiding Programmer Burnout

Preface

Is this book for you?

This book is for anyone interested in a career as a software engineer. Whether you are looking to get that elusive first software engineering job or upgrade to better one. This book will provide you with the steps to work and progress as a software engineer.

Having personally experienced and watched others go through the process of having zero programming experience, to landing their first job as a software engineer, I have firsthand experience of the steps that need to be taken.

The book also details my journey as an assistant nurse who knew nothing about coding, to now having worked nearly two years, as a software engineer. It also contains stories from my own journey which will hopefully provide inspiration and motivation.

Although this is a how to book, on landing a software engineering job. The book is intended to be a guide rather than academic publication and should not be taken as gospel. Also, to ensure the material in this book is useful in the long term, efforts have been made to avoid material that is subject to change, such as software languages and coding syntax.

This book contains an overview of fundamental topics you will need to learn, to become a software engineer, however, it does not go into enough detail to know them proficiently. So, it's best to learn these topics from other materials which I provide recommendations for, throughout the book.

What is a self-taught software engineer?

A 'self-taught' software engineer is considered someone who has taught himself to be proficient enough at developing software, to be hired to do it professionally.

Within the software development community there is a debate on the difference between a 'software engineer' and a 'software developer'. However, since there isn't a strict definition for either, in this book we will use both to mean, someone who designs, architects and develops software professionally.

Software companies hiring software engineers tend to look more favourably on candidates who have computer science degrees. Because of this, those without degrees, typically find it harder to break into the industry, which is one of the problems this book will attempt to solve.

This book can be useful to those who want to attain or already have a computer science degree, because this book contains strategies, mindsets, habits and concepts which will enable you to land a job as a software engineer and are unlikely to be taught in a traditional computer science degree programs.

Chapter 1: Assistant Nurse to Software Engineer

"When something is important enough, you do it even if the odds are not in your favour" - Elon Musk

Working as an assistant nurse

After finishing my undergraduate studies, I travelled to the north of England to work in a hospital ward as an assistant nurse. I was hoping this experience would allow me to work alongside medical doctors to determine if a career in medicine was for me.

Working as an assistant nurse was not a glamorous job and although I decided against a career in medicine, the experience taught me valuable communication and soft skills that helped me in my role as a software engineer.

My time working as an assistant Nurse ended after nine months, and I decided to travel to Asia, which is where my journey to becoming a software engineer began.

It was during this time, I had the chance to read 'Elon Musk: How the Billionaire CEO of SpaceX and Tesla is Shaping our Future'. The book details how Elon Musk had built and sold various software during the dot com bubble, but the most intriguing part was after teaching himself to code, he developed the software needed to create PayPal, an online payment system.

Most popular careers such as law and medicine require decades of study, practice as well as getting through the endless amounts of bureaucracy before finally getting to the higher tier positions where one can have a major impact. Whereas in software development, it's largely in one's own hands, as Elon Musk demonstrated by building PayPal.

After reading the book, I thought the ability to build software was a modern-day superpower, and I wanted to learn how to do it. I had always had an interest in computers and enjoyed using MATLAB (programming language) at university, however the idea of building software as a career had never occurred to me.

One day, I spoke to my colleague about my desire to learn to code. He mentioned there was a school nearby offering an evening JavaScript course. I signed up to the course, and the first lesson was an introduction to JavaScript.

As the weeks went by, the material in the class got tougher. We were practicing sorting arrays, using prototypes and much more. By far, I was the worst student in the class, and although my teachers were patient, it was clear I was getting on their nerves with my poor coding abilities.

Every week students would drop out, but I forced myself to keep showing up. Despite not understanding the material being taught. However, by the end of the course I had a sense that software development was the right career for me. A few months later, I would redo this course later on and perform much better.

The customer support role

Whilst attending the JavaScript evening classes at the coding school, I came across an advertisement for a full-time position in a technical customer support role for a e-commerce start-up. I interviewed for the role and was accepted. The salary was not enough to live on, and I was initially paid three dollars and twenty-three cents per hour. This forced me to use my savings and live very frugally.

My main reason for taking this role was that I would get the chance to practice web development. The role would also give me entry into a tech company, and a chance to achieve my dream of working professionally as a software engineer.

The customer support role continued for eight months, where I learnt to customize tens of thousands of ecommerce themes using various programming languages. The job also gave me the opportunity to work with other engineers on the team whom I learned a lot from. Overall it was a tremendous learning experience.

Coding boot camp experience

After eight months of working in the customer support role, I received a call from the school where I took the evening JavaScript classes, letting me know they were going to hold an intensive Full Stack Software Development Bootcamp.

It would run every day from morning to evening on weekdays. It would cover front-end languages, backend languages and even how to manipulate databases using SQL. There was also a guaranteed software engineer job if we were to complete the boot camp. So, I gathered up all my remaining savings and signed up for the boot camp.

The first day, I looked around the class and there were eighteen students. At that moment, I promised I would work harder than anyone else in the class. The classes lasted for nine hours, but I often stayed after class for another three hours, working on assignments that had been set.

During the boot camp I continued working as a part time customer support agent for the start-up to help pay for my living expenses. For those three months I would start class at nine in the morning and would often finish at eleven at night. This meant I would spend between twelve to fourteen hours per day on the computer, which is a decision I would later regret.

The coding boot camp classes were intense, every morning we would learn fundamental skills and concepts to build software. Most days we were given a project to complete for the next day. Some days this meant staying up until midnight, coding to meet the deadline which was due the next day. After the first month of the coding boot camp, half the class had dropped out.

After the first month, we started to learn backend development which I hadn't learnt before, as I had been primarily focused on front-end languages. This is where the learning really began for me. The lectures on backend development were on a range of topics such as databases, background processing and caching. We used the popular Python programming language to build our projects and we even built an app that would read out information from the web to blind people.

At various times during the course, we would receive guest lecturers from software engineers who worked in big companies such as Facebook, Google and Oracle, which was informative. When the coding boot camp was nearly at its end, there were just six other students including myself.

However, some of the other students were not taking the boot camp seriously but because I wanted to become a software engineer, I kept to myself and focused on learning. Our final project was to build a full stack application and present it to the class. The best three presentations would get the opportunity to present to a panel of judges, with the winner receiving a prize.

I built an application called 'E-shop Health Check' an automated testing tool for e-commerce stores that takes daily screenshots of the checkout process. It used React JS on the front end and Python on the backend. My app landed me a place in the finale.

The night before the final, I had stayed awake most of the night to complete a final feature. Despite my efforts, I did not win the competition. However, the start-up I worked in a customer support position for, came to the competition and offered me a position as a trainee software engineer.

As a trainee software engineer, I would undergo an internal training program, where I would receive mentoring sessions twice a week and once completed, would be hired as a full stack software engineer. After eleven months of hard work, finally I had my opportunity.

Landing a job as a software engineer

After the coding boot camp ended I began my role as a trainee software engineer. This meant performing my regular duties as a customer support representative, alongside studying the material the company prepared for me to become a software engineer.

Twice a week, there would be mentorship sessions with the CTO (chief technical officer) of the company. We covered a comprehensive list of software engineering concepts, only in much more detail than in the coding boot camp. Every day, after finishing work, I'd go home and revise what I had learnt that day.

After 5 months in my role as a trainee software engineer, I was finally given the title of 'Full Stack Software Engineer'. In total it had taken thirteen months of intensive practice which included three months of self-study, four months at coding boot camp and five months as a trainee software engineer.

The journey from knowing nothing about software to eventually being hired to build software as a profession was one of the hardest, yet enjoyable experiences and includes many fond memories.

Chapter 2: Is Software Engineering the Right Career Path for You?

"Optimism is an occupational hazard of programming: feedback is the treatment.*" - Kent Beck*

When considering a career in software development, it's helpful to understand what the job entails. This chapter will detail some of the key parts of a software engineer's role to help determine if a career in software engineering is even for you.

The joy of coding

The vast majority of a software engineer's time is spent coding. This means communicating instructions to the computer in creative ways to perform specific tasks. Contrary to popular belief writing computer programs is a creative process and often appeals to those with a creative side.

The creativity in programming is related to how a problem is solved. When coding, if we use the first solution we arrive at, this is not creative, however if we take a step back and look at all the possible solutions, this is when the creative process can begin.

Computers take a set of instructions from the code written by a programmer. A creative programmer can pick the best set of instructions to improve the performance, prevent bugs and make it easier to add future functionality to these instructions. For example, a programmer may be given a choice between two algorithms.

Initially he uses algorithm A, but upon investigating further he discovers Algorithm B performs better in the context he's using it in. When we start to look for ways to optimize code, this is where coding can become very creative.

Coding is for the most part a problem-solving activity and as a result requires concentrating for long periods of time. Good software engineers look at problems with fascination and are eager to solve it. When they eventually solve a problem, they feel a sense of pride and accomplishment, whereas most would be just happy it is fixed and move on.

Coding requires a large degree of patience and persistence because you may spend days trying to solve a small problem, only to find you missed one coding character.

If you're the type of person who doesn't enjoy problem solving, creativity and gets frustrated easily, you most likely won't enjoy coding and thus a career developing software, isn't for you.

Staring at computer screens

This might seem obvious but a significant portion of a software engineer's time is spent staring at a computer screen. So, if you do not enjoy using computers, this isn't the career for you.

Since I've been working as a software engineer, I spend at least eight to nine hours a day staring at the computer screen. A large proportion of this time is spent coding which includes during and after working hours, because improving your skills outside of work is important to progress as a software engineer.

Also, coding is a mentally fatiguing activity because it involves 'mental modelling'. Reading and writing code is synonymous with a flow chart, for example; A triggers B which triggers C, but C is only triggered when F is 1.

Each letter can be thought of as an 'event', and in a single feature there can be hundreds of these events. If there is a bug, an engineer will go through this mental model by looking through the code to find out which event caused the bug.

A software engineer is expected to spend a considerable amount of their daily life staring at the computer screen and solving problems. So, the question one needs to ask themselves is when considering this career path is; will you be happy staring at a computer screen and creatively solving problems for most of your working hours?

Red tape

As a software engineer, your main role is to develop software for a user. When building features, an engineer may have input on how the feature looks and functions, but it is typically the project manager who has the final say.

Furthermore, software engineers have little control over which and when features are built, this again is handled by managers. Although senior engineers have more of a say it is unlikely they will have complete creative control.

In software companies, there are typically teams of people involved in the production of software. This could include UX/UI designers, QA testers, project managers, branding and marketing. For this reason, even though a feature has been built, it might need approval from other teams before it is allowed to be pushed live. Sometimes this could mean a feature being in the backlog for long periods of time.

Intelligence

Like any challenging career, working as a software engineer does require a level of intelligence. It is hard to define intelligence but as of right now the closest we have come to defining it, is using the infamous IQ test.

According to occupational IQ studies the average IQ range for a software engineer is between 110-120 IQ points [1], however if your IQ is below that, don't let this stop you because hard work can be used to compensate. For example, if an individual score a 100 in an IQ test, it is certainly possible for them to achieve the results of an individual who scored 140 IQ through hard work.

A large proportion of a software engineer's time is dedicated to "thinking" about piecing code together and the possible results of piecing them together in that particular way. As you can probably imagine, this takes a degree of intelligence. However, with persistence and patience, in my opinion landing a role as a software engineer is possible for almost everyone.

He who has a why can bear almost any how

Whether it is love of problem solving, computers or building a greater tomorrow. Having a reason for working as a software engineer will help you get through the tough times.

These tough times are especially present, if you do not have a traditional education in software development, because the road to getting that first job will generally be longer and harder compared to those who already have a computer science degree. My reason for pursuing software development was to build software to help people.

Skills and characteristics of a software engineer

When contemplating a career in software development, it's useful to know skills and traits of individuals who typically work as software engineers. Software engineers come in various forms but there are certain characteristics and skills that are common amongst software engineers.

And although they are not essential, by working on improving these skills and traits you increase the likelihood of becoming a better software engineer. In the following paragraphs I will outline these traits and skills along with examples.

In high school, my mathematics grades were average, however I really enjoyed solving the various problems the subject has to offer. I especially enjoyed solving a problem, if I knew it was going to help someone else.

A large proportion of a software engineer's time is dedicated to problem solving for users. This involves solving problems using code, as well as logistical and human problems. For example, deciding on the software deployment flow or the best framework to use for a given feature. For this reason, being a good at or enjoying problem solver is necessary as a software engineer.

When building complicated software, inevitably you will run into a problem that cannot be solved instantly. Solving this problem may take longer than expected. For this reason, being persistent and patient are important traits of any software engineer. There have been plenty of occasions where I encountered a problem that I initially thought was unsolvable, but through persistence and patience, it was eventually solved.

In the beginning every problem is viewed as a difficult task but as you become more experienced every problem has a multitude of solutions and the question becomes which solution is most suitable rather than what is the solution. To develop software, a high degree of persistence will be needed, as inevitably you will run into bugs that might take hours or even days to solve.

Chapter 3: Avoiding Burnout and Practices to Stay Healthy as a Software Engineer

"Burnout is what happens when you try to avoid being human for too long" - Michael Gungot

Burnout is a syndrome that occurs as a result of chronic work-place stress that has not been managed correctly according to the World Health organization [2].

It is common for software engineers to experience burnout. There are numerous factors that can contribute to burnout which include workplace culture, lack of meaning in work and personal beliefs or mindsets. Common symptoms associated with burnout include a lack of motivation, irritability and cynicism.

My experience with programmer burnout

After nearly a year of working as a full-time software engineer, I had started to experience migraines and eye aches, which would typically occur after long periods of coding, as a result of staring at the computer screen. Also, I had started to experience severe pain in my finger joints to the point where sleeping became difficult. It got so bad, I would put my hands in a bowl of ice after a day's work to reduce the pain.

At the time I adopted the mindset of pushing through the pain, which had worked for me in previous ventures. However, I discovered my hand pain was as a result of a repetitive strain injury in my finger joints because of excessive use of the computer's trackpad when coding. And finally, there was the stress and generally feeling of being miserable, I had not experienced prior to becoming a software engineer.

Whilst working as a software engineer, I would spend my days working a 9-6 job and spending the evenings building side projects. This could mean spending up to twelve hours a day, coding. Combined with coding boot camp and self-taught studying I spent six thousand hours learning to code within eighteen months.

It became apparent I was burning out, when I became very cynical and lacked the motivation to work on projects outside of work, which I previously enjoyed. Finally, one night, after working until midnight, I woke up in a pool of sweat with racing thoughts. I was having a panic attack. After this I took a break from coding for a period of time, to recover.

The mental and emotional health problems associated with burnout are well documented within the software development community. However less well known are the physical induced health problems associated with burnout due to excessive computer usage. The physical health problems range from skeletal disorders such as the infamous 'computer back', muscular injuries and eye strain.

The repetitive strain injury I had experienced in my finger joints were relatively minor and thankfully I recovered. However, there are plenty of lessons that I took away from my burnout experience that I will share in the upcoming paragraphs, so that you do not make the same mistakes I made.

Setup and burnout preventatives

Having the correct tooling, for software engineers, is an important factor to prevent burnout and physical injury. Below are some I would consider getting if you are planning on coding on a daily basis in order to prevent computer induced health problems.

Ergonomic mouse

Using a normal mouse or a trackpad forces the muscles in your hand and wrist to make repetitive, focused movements which overuse the same small muscles causing musculoskeletal disorders. Having experienced muscular injuries in finger joints due to excessive trackpad usage, and after switching over to the ergonomic mouse it made a massive difference in my recovery.

By using an ergonomic mouse from the start, it will prevent yourself from suffering repetitive strain injuries (RSI) in the hand which are not uncommon in software development. I would recommend using the **ZLOT vertical wireless ergonomic mouse**.

Ergonomic Chair

As a software engineer, most of your job will be spent sitting on a chair. Prolonged sitting and poor posture can lead to the infamous 'computer back' or even more severe spinal disc injuries. The best solution is to invest in an ergonomic chair with lumbar support.

Protecting eyes

Eyestrain is a common symptom for those who spend excessive time on the computer. This can later progress to computer vision syndrome, which can require medical treatment. Having personally experienced eyestrain, due to excessive computer use, there are few suggestions I would make.

The first being, limiting the screen time outside of work. By doing this you allow your body and mind to recover. The other recommendation would be to use anti-glare glasses and ensure eye-care mode is enabled on your monitor, which adds an additional layer of protection and prevents your eyes from absorbing blue light, reducing sleep loss [3].

Exercising and stretching

We all know regular exercise is important for general well-being. However, for a software engineer exercise can be more important, because the job demands high cognitive ability, stress resilience and concentration which are all improved through regular exercise. Research has demonstrated regular aerobic based exercises, improved cognitive ability. Which could be the reason for the CEO's of the FAANG (Facebook, Amazon, Apple, Netflix, Google) companies being avid runners.

Stretching is another exercise I have regularly taken part in after becoming a software engineer. This is to prevent the dreaded computer hunchback and long-term back problems due to sitting on a chair all day. A popular stretch that can be used to correct posture, whilst you are at your desk, is the '**Bruggers Relief Position**'[4]. This position is a great way to reduce back and neck pain, it only takes six seconds.

Healthy Lifestyle

Having a healthy lifestyle is vital for longevity in any career but especially in the field of software development because it can be a very stressful job. To reduce stress, various measures can be taken, such as exercise, avoiding junk food and socialising.

A common stereotype for programmers are individuals who lack social skills and are generally loners. There are numerous studies which suggest there is a strong association with loneliness and cognitive decline [5]. So, by avoiding loneliness and being social we can reach our fullest cognitive ability, reduce stress and become a more productive software engineer.

Communication

An often-overlooked part of avoiding burnout, is to communicate with others when you are experiencing burnout type symptoms. It is often the case that software engineers get so lost in the coding process, that they ignore fatigue and battle through.

By catching your burnout symptoms early and letting others know, they could give you advice on the course of action to take. If you're already working as a software engineer this could involve letting your project manager and if you do not, friends and family.

Don't be a hero

If you're working on a large project, it will inevitably take time. For this reason, it's important to view the project as a marathon and not a sprint. By having this mindset, you will be able to set a pace that will not result in you having to go into 'hackathon mode' which will result in burning out faster.

Part of setting the pace is to set realistic deadlines with yourself and the person you are reporting to. Adding extra buffer time for bugs that will inevitably occur is always advisable.

To prevent burnout, it is useful to know when to quit. Often when software engineers cannot solve a problem, they think spending more time on it is the best solution. However sometimes it may be best to just ask others for help or take a break.

It's not uncommon to come up with the solution to a problem whilst not thinking about it, because it allows your unconscious brain to work on the problem, which is often the reason for an 'aha' moment [6].

Setting the pace also refers to work you may do outside of normal working hours. Non-working hours should be used to recover and recuperate, and not for additional work. By setting rules such as not taking your work home you will give your body enough time to recover in preparation for the next working day.

Most software engineers work on side projects outside of work. If this is the case, then setting a time limit on computer usage outside of your work, could be beneficial to prevent computer induced health problems.

Research has shown staring at computer screens before going to bed, prevents high quality sleep [7] because the blue light that is emitted from the screen makes it more difficult to fall asleep. By cutting off screen time two hours prior to bed, the body will be more prepared to fall into deep REM (rapid eye movement) sleep which is needed for the body to fully recuperate.

Why is there so much burnout amongst software engineers?

Burnout can affect everyone; this needs to be understood. Presenting as exhaustion that spans the emotional, mental, and physical domains of the human psyche, it is typically caused by excessive stress levels that are due to long hours, inhumane amounts of caffeine, and a lack of sleep.

Software engineers tend to fall into this burnout trap as their days are filled with meetings and acting on the outcomes of that day's meetings. According to research apart from doctors, software engineers have one of the most irregular sleeping schedules [8].

Burnout can be caused when you have lost the excitement of a project but have to continue it with an absence of reward, agency, and recovery. As you relentlessly work on this project, your end goal is to finish it, no matter the cost.

This mentality is extremely common within the context of a software engineer. The result of this is an unbalanced lifestyle that includes a lack of exercise, poor mental health, unhealthy food choices, diminishing self-care, and no time to unwind and perform actions that you enjoy.

In this context, software engineers need to be cognizant of burnout's realness. They also should be able to strategically delineate what burnout is not. Having burnout does not mean that you are lazy, have ADHD, or are depressed. But why does the software development space have this extreme burden of burnout occurrence? The answer is rather simple.

Software engineering has no boundaries. With software engineering, there are no set hours that you are required to reach deadlines in, the direction of your project can rapidly change, and the loneliness associated with remote work hinders social interactions and leads to you bottling up all your stress, unrest, and anxiety.

So, how do you treat and prevent burnout? The approach is a holistic one. In order to stave off burnout, you will want to ensure that you are not only addressing the root cause of the burnout from a work perspective, but that you are giving your body the love it needs whilst cultivating those socially beneficial human relationships. Exercise and eating healthy release endorphins, which are chemicals in your brain that make you feel happy about yourself and your actions.

This with a good eight hours of sleep will leave you feeling refreshed and energized to tackle your work day without needing to fear any impending burnout that may be waiting for you. It is important that you are open with your employer about any burnout symptoms that you are experiencing. The worst thing you can do is keep it all bottled up, because when that bottle bursts, your psyche will be hit a lot harder.

Burnout is real, and once you begin to acknowledge its presence, where it can manifest, as well as how to prevent it, you will begin to realize that your productivity levels will increase. Being a software engineer comes with many different and unique stresses, and these stresses need to be rectified if you are going to continue growing in your trade. They will also help you to not succumb to any hint of burnout should it present itself.

Improving communication skills as a software engineer

Communication as a software developer is one of the most important aspects of the job. In order for you to effectively understand what is required of you, whether in the corporate world or based on a personal project, you need to be a good communicator. This is why it is always vital that you dedicate some time to learning this skill, what constitutes good communication, and how some communication can be seen as offensive. You want to ensure that there is a well-rounded partnership with your co-workers or customers. Good communication will always enhance this partnership.

One of the best ways to master the art of communication is to learn how to listen effectively and with intent to what your customers or co-workers are saying [9]. Listening without coming to assumptions is not as easy as it sounds.

For instance, let's say your employer asks you to create a website to show what encompasses guerrilla warfare. If you heard "gorilla" and jumped to the conclusion that you would be focusing on the animal instead of the war tactic, you will be wasting your own and the company's time and resources.

However, if you were to listen intently and until the end of the conversation, you may have found that your employer also wanted the historical significance of guerrilla warfare. This extra bit of listening will save you time since you won't have to ask questions later. It will also possibly save you some backlash received from the employer as he/she now needs to repeat himself/herself.

Fear is the greatest paralysing force, forcing us to believe that we are not strong enough nor capable of being able to communicate effectively. Whether it be the status of another individual or what you have heard about them, the thought of communicating with a specific individual may seem rather daunting. However, if you are able to harness this fear and analyse what it is that is causing it, you should have the ability to remove the problem by the root.

Focusing on your fears when communicating will cause you to stumble over your words, losing the core message behind them. For example, let us imagine that a country's president is consulting your company to do a project.

You now need to talk to the president to detail what it is that is required. You may fear that you will say something wrong or inappropriate, or that the questions you are asking are too obvious. However, if you focus on the meaning of what you want to say rather than how you might sound saying it, you will portray knowledge and understanding of the project.

A good communicator requires knowledge of a wide range of topics. Depending on who you may be communicating with, the category of knowledge and the depth required will differ. You cannot communicate effectively on a topic that you do not understand. This is why it's so important to continue learning, both within and outside of your craft's domain.

Chapter 4: The self-taught software engineer mind frames and habits

"The most important question anyone can ask is; what myth am I living in?"

- Carl Jung

Unless you are fortunate, the journey to landing that first software engineer job will be a long and difficult road. My own journey to my first job as a software engineer, was a long one with plenty of sacrifices. The main reason for it being so difficult, is as a self-taught engineer you lack the qualifications to demonstrate your skills and willingness to work in software development. And for this reason, some employers may automatically dismiss you.

As with any challenging goal, having certain mindsets can help you to take the necessary actions to achieve your goal. Creating beneficial mind frames, will allow you to take the correct actions to accomplish your goal. The mind frames that you create can be thought of as your own way of looking at the world or in the words of Carl Jung the *"myth you are living in"*. If you have been successful in other areas of your life, it's likely you already have an idea of the mind frames necessary to achieve a goal.

I first understood mind frames, after reading the book **'Awaken the Giant Within'**. From that moment forward, I used frames and have adapted my own frames whilst learning and writing code. Below are the frames I have created and found most helpful as a software engineer:

- *Every bug or mistake is an opportunity to learn.*
- *I'm not the best programmer in the world and that's fine. I just want to be a better programmer than I was yesterday.*
- *Write code in a way, my future self would want to read it.*
- *Long term results are more important than how I feel in this present moment.*
- *I will not judge myself for failing to reach goals that are not in my control.*

- *Programming knowledge is to be treasured and memorized, wherever it comes from.*
- *I will focus on understanding concepts rather than memorized syntax.*

I have found reading these frames out loud helped to embed them into my mind. So, when faced with a problem, dilemma in a pressure situation, the above frames helped me decide the best course of action.

10,000 hours

Everyone is in such a rush to get results. Learning to build software is no exception and this is evident when looking at titles of popular programming books and online courses such as "Teach yourself Java in 24 hours" and "Learn Python in 24 hours".

It is near impossible to build several sophisticated software projects to learn from or understand the inner workings of language within a twenty-four-hour period. On the other hand, it is possible to learn the basic syntax of a software language to accomplish a task but this is not programming, so unfortunately teaching yourself to be proficient in a software language within twenty-four hours, is just not possible.

The popular 10,000-hour rule found in Outliers [13] by Malcom Gladwell, mentions it takes an individual ten thousand hours of deliberate practice to be a master in their field. Researchers have found it takes about ten years to develop an expertise in a variety of different fields including swimming, tennis, painting, piano playing and music playing.

Of course, expertise in a field depends on various other factors and so it will not take exactly ten thousand hours to become an expert. Rather, the ten-thousand-hour rule is an indicator that it takes a long time to become a master in a field, such as software engineering.

It's also important to note the ten-thousand-hour rule is predicated on deliberate practice, which is challenging yourself to a task which is slightly beyond your ability, rather than doing the same task repeatedly. Also, the ten-thousand-hour rule is for achieving mastery, but you do not need to write software for ten thousand hours to land your first software engineering job.

The popular online www.freecodecamp.org course has had thousands of students complete their courses who after finishing the course, go on to land software engineering jobs. Their material for learning both the front-end and back-end of software development takes around three thousand hours.

However, if one dedicated their time to learning just the front-end or back-end development, it would take one thousand five hundred hours before being proficient enough to land a job. This means dedicating around three and half hours to learning either front-end or back-end development every day, for a year and three months.

It is also important to note that software engineering as a career requires a lifetime of learning and practice. This means, practicing and learning is necessary to stay up to date with the latest technologies and continue to improve one's programming abilities.

Repetition is the mother of learning

Developing the skills to become a hireable software engineer requires understanding, research and practice of core software engineer skills. For example, understanding the concept of looping through data and then the practice of looping through various data structures using various loops.

By repeatedly practicing looping through data, you will expose yourself to various scenarios, providing the reference experience you will need to loop through data when you develop software professionally.

Another benefit of continuous practice is that sometimes a concept doesn't make much sense on first reading. But through repeated practice of the concept you are able to understand the various components of the concept and it becomes understandable. For example, the first time I learned about an API (Application Programming Interface), it did not make much sense until I actually built an API.

Follow through

There are numerous research papers showing that by writing down your goals, a personal is more likely to achieve [14]. I would even go a step further by visualising and read my goals out loud every day.

For myself, writing down daily, weekly, quarterly and yearly goals have been instrumental in switching to a career in software development. My daily goal was to code two to three hours per day, whilst my monthly and year goals were used for larger projects and landing my first software engineer job.

It is important, to realize, contrary to popular belief, software development isn't a skill that can be picked up in a few days, weeks or months. From my experience watching others learning to code, the average person will generally take between twelve to eighteen months to learn the necessary skills to be hireable.

This is provided you study and practice on a consistent basis, from my experience for an average person it will take at least two to four hours of coding per day, to become reasonably skilled enough to land a role within a twelve to eighteen-month period.

By setting yourself daily targets, monthly and yearly targets, you not only increase the chances of landing your first software engineer job but also develop the habit of coding everyday which is vital to levelling up your programming skills, once you get the job and beyond.

Memorization

Software development is an enormous field with various technologies, frameworks and concepts to understand. For this reason, it is important to be able to learn and pick up new concepts, relatively quickly.

When learning software development fundamentals, it is important to not only understand the concept you are learning but also memorize it, because it is possible to be asked questions about them during an interview but also it will help shape your habits and practices as a software engineer.

The memorization method that has served me well, has been using a flashcard tool such as ANKI [10]. This tool utilizes spaced repetition, which is a method used to increase the rate of memorization. Doing memorization card sessions, will allow you to retain the much-needed software development fundamentals needed to excel at interviews and throughout your career.

It is important not to waste time memorizing specific coding syntax as this will most likely change, and seek to only keep information that will be present throughout your career.

Persistence and resilience

Unless you are fortunate, getting that first software engineer will require a high level of persistence, especially if you do not have a university education in computer science. The level of persistence required varies according to an individual's situation, however it could mean sending out a thousand job applications or working late to finish an important assignment.

I spent thousands of hours learning to code. Each day I forced myself to spend at least two hours per day coding, no matter how I felt. For eighteen months, there wasn't a day that went by where I didn't reach my daily goal of coding two hours per day.

By forcing yourself to code, even when you do not want to, you are building the 'persistence muscle', which will allow you to code even when you are not feeling inspired or motivated. I cannot tell you how many times, I initially thought a software engineering problem was too difficult for me to solve, however by exercising my 'persistence muscle' and putting one foot in front of the other, the problem became solvable.

Deep work

One of the most important skills a software engineer can possess, is the ability to do deep work. This is the ability to focus deeply for long periods of time, which allows you to push your cognitive abilities to the limit, quickly pick up complex information and as a result create better software. Unfortunately, today's world is full of distractions, which makes it difficult to achieve deep work.

The author Cal Newport in his book Deep Work, highlights that an expert can go into deep work for around four hours per day whilst a novice can only manage one hour [11]. This indicates that experts have developed the skill of deep focus over time and that the time spent in deep work can be increased with practice.

To start deploying deep work into your life, you will need to start eliminating distractions. This can be done through quitting social media or other distracting websites, especially during periods of deep work. Software engineers spend most of their time on the computer, so it is always tempting to browse the web, so using tools to block unproductive sites can prevent being distracted during deep work.

It is also helpful to schedule periods in the day where you will work deeply and remove all distractions in this period (including phone calls and emails), and use tools such as KanbanFlow [12] are great for scheduling. I have found moving the most mentally intensive tasks to these deep work periods, and using the rest of my time for less mentally demanding tasks.

Domain knowledge

In the business world, software engineers are required to build software that ultimately helps the business bring in revenue. However, if a software engineer does not have domain knowledge which means an understanding of what the company does or the direction they are heading in, it can cause incorrect implementations of features and incorrect prioritization of tasks and as a result, a loss in revenue.

For this reason, it's useful for software engineers to have a basic understanding of the business they are working in, specifically what the business does, it's motivations and mission statements.

When coding a feature, it's useful for a software engineer to have a higher business goal in mind. This enables an engineer to see the possible edge cases, prioritize and build code to handle them if required.

Also, by understanding the needs of the company, software engineers know what needs to be done, which will prevent endless feedback loops where engineers have to constantly get approval of the company before making changes. Additionally, when scoping out a new project software engineers should also ask lots of questions to fully understand the requirements of the feature.

As a software engineer, having domain knowledge makes your job more meaningful as you will better understand the benefits of the code you write. For example, building colour swatches on an online fashion store so customers can more easily shop. It is not necessary to have extensive knowledge of the domain you are working in, however it's useful to have enough domain knowledge to understand the impact features on the business, as this will help to craft the implementation of these features.

Dress sense

First impressions matter, whether we like or not people will judge others by their appearance. A little while ago, I worked for a start-up, and dressed in stereotypical software engineer attire (hoodie, jeans and trainers). Whilst this was satisfactory for my environment, I noticed the senior developers and upper management would dress noticeably smarter than the junior developers and members in the lower half of the work hierarchy.

When I started to dress smarter at work, there was a noticeable improvement in the way people at work treated me. This was not because my colleagues were judgemental! Rather it is a survival mechanism, humans have used for thousands of years. Which is the ability to stereotype or make a quick judgement on a person. This survival mechanism has helped humans to detect enemies and allies. Similarly, if we see someone dressing better or similar to us, we assume he is a friend and therefore trustworthy.

We've all heard the phrase "Dress for success", and research by Scientific America has shown that the clothing you wear actually improves abstract thinking, big picture thinking and focus [14], which are useful skills when programming. This indicates the clothing one wears can also impact performance. With remote work becoming ever more common, it is tempting to work in the attire you woke up in, however by dressing as if you are going to the office, you are likely to see a productivity and performance improvement.

Healthy dose of scepticism

One of the common traits of a good software engineer, is they are inherently sceptical. This means applying reason to all ideas that are presented and questioning everything. Only code, tests, documentation and specification are considered believable. Whilst this attitude might seem pessimistic, it helps to prevent mistakes in software which could be extremely costly.

A healthy dose of scepticism helps to prevent a decision being made based on authority, friendship, position or current trends. For example, a non-technical project manager requests to change the software stack for a project because it will help to roll out features faster based on popular articles the manager found online. A sceptical software engineer questions these assumptions and through deliberate research finds changing the stack will have actually little to no effect on the feature roll out speed.

If the software engineer accepted the decision from authority and had gone ahead with the decision to change the software stack, it would have cost the company resources for little benefit. By being sceptical a software engineer can prevent costly mistakes, improve code quality and as result produce better software.

Divide and conquer

In computer science, the divide and conquer approach is an algorithm design paradigm and is the basis for many algorithms that solves problems such as sorting algorithms. It is also a useful approach to problems in software development as it enables the breaking down of a complicated problem into its sub problems, until those sub problems become solvable. The solutions to all these sub problems are then merged together to solve the original problem.

Splitting a problem into smaller parts is commonly applied in software development by writing pseudocode, which is the plain language description of the code which can be more easily understood. This divide and conquer approach is beautifully summarised by the philosopher Rene Descartes who said *"Divide each difficulty into as many parts as is feasible and necessary to resolve it"*.

Paying yourself first

As someone who's eager to learn software development but has other responsibilities, it can be difficult to schedule time to learn. If that's the case, I would recommend adopting the mindset of paying yourself first, which means doing the things that will help you reach your most important goal, at the very beginning of the day. This could mean waking up an hour or two earlier to learn software development or even work on improving your CV for job applications.

Research has indicated, people are most productive at the start of the day [15], and by utilizing this time to work on the most important goal, they progress with this goal faster than if they were to work on their goal at the end of the day. For this reason, to achieve your goal of working as a software engineer, it's most productive to pay yourself first.

Chapter 5: The self-taught software engineer coding roadmap

"Whether you want to uncover the secrets of the universe, or you just want to pursue a career in the 21st century, basic computer programming is an essential skill to learn." - Stephen Hawking

As an applicant for a role as a software engineer, the main factor that will determine landing that first role, is the skills you possess as well as the ability to demonstrate those skills. In this chapter we will go through the topics and concepts you will need to learn to be able to get your coding skills up to a level where you will be job ready.

This chapter contains general principles of the topics and does not include an in-detail explanation of the topics, coding exercises or coding syntax. There are two reasons for this, the first is the syntax and specific details of a topic will likely evolve however the general principle will most likely stay the same and the second is this book would be very long if all the details and syntax were included.

Create a learning plan

Before starting to learn and practice the necessary skills to become a software engineer, you must first decide what type of software engineer you would like to become? Feel free to skip ahead to Chapter 7 where the major career paths of a software engineer are described. But do not worry, it is possible to switch to a different career path within software engineering at a later point.

Once you've decided on the type of software engineer you would like become, it's necessary to create a list of topics and skills that you would need to learn to become proficient in that software engineering career path. In the following sections below is a coding roadmap that covers the key topics that are necessary to become a software engineer.

Now we have the list of topics we need to learn, it's now time to create a timetable that will dictate the daily actions you are going to take to learn these topics. Ideally you want to be studying at least two to three hours per day. Use tools like Google calendar to schedule your daily learnings and using time management techniques such as Pomodoro sessions to aid in optimizing the time spent learning.

The trifecta of building websites

Since 1995 websites, websites have been built using HTML, CSS and JavaScript. It is essential for any software engineer to have a basic understanding of these languages. Typically learning HTML and CSS is best, before going onto learning JavaScript.

CSS (Cascading Stylesheet)

Allows styling and positioning of elements on a webpage. For example, changing colour or font of elements.

HTML (Hypertext Mark-up Language)

Defines the structure or skeleton of a webpage. It tells the browser what type of content is being displayed, for example, it tells the browser "this is an image".

Vanilla JavaScript

A scripting language that allows for dynamic functionality like auto completing text, loading data on a page without refreshing or adding effects based on user input.

If you are planning on becoming a front-end software engineer, learning the trifecta of front-end developer languages is just the start. Nowadays you will be also expected to understand and implement web standards and best practices such as:

- Accessibility on the web
- Cross browser compatibility
- SEO (search engine optimization)
- Web security and vulnerabilities:
  - XSS (Cross site scripting)
  - CSRF attacks (Cross-Site Request Forgery)
- Cookies, sessions and local storage
- Improving page load time and website performance

Comparison, logical and arithmetic operators

In programming an operator is a symbol that determines what action is to be performed. There are three main types of operators: arithmetic, logic and comparison.

Arithmetic operators

These are mathematical functions that are used to perform calculations on specific values e.g. minus, add, subtract and divide.

Arithmetic operation	Operator	Usage
Addition	+	y = y + 2
Subtraction	-	y = y - 2
Division	/	y = y/2
Multiplication	*	y = y*2
Remainder	%	y = 3%2

Table 1. Arithmetic operators with examples

Logical Operators

A logical operator can be a symbol or word, which is used to join two or more expressions together to produce a compound expression. The most common logical operators are AND, OR and NOT.

Logical operation	Operator	Usage
AND	&&	x && y
OR	||	x || y
NOT	!	!= x

Table 2. Logical operators with examples (these operators are used by most programming languages but not all)

Comparison Operators

These operators are used in logical expressions to determine the equality or difference between values.

Comparison operation	Operator	Usage
Equal to	==	x == y
Equal value and type	===	x === y
Not equal to	!=	x != y
Greater than	>	x > y

Less than	<	x < y
Greater than and equal to	>=	x >= y
Less than and equal to	<=	x <= y

Data Structures

Data structures are specific layouts that hold data. Most applications or websites hold large amounts of data in a database. Let's say this data is from an e-commerce site and includes order information for users and a user attempts to view their order history on an e-commerce website.

The website will send a request to the server which will look up the users order history in the database. When the order information is retrieved, it will be placed in a data structure that will hold the data, which will be outputted to the user.

The question for a programmer is which data structure to use to hold the data. There are lots of different kinds of data structures, each with their own strengths and weaknesses. Below are the eight most common data structures:

- Arrays
- Stacks
- Queues
- Linked list
- Trees
- Graphs
- Tries
- Hash tables

It is unlikely you will encounter all these data structures whilst coding, however it is useful to at least know and understand all of them in case you are asked about them during an interview. The most common data structure is an array and we will cover it in more detail below.

Array

An array is a series of memory locations which each hold a single item of data. An array is capable of holding multiple items. The main benefit of an array, is that the values can be easily sorted and searched.

Each item in an array can be identified using its index which is an items position in the array. An index starts off from zero and increments by one, so the index value of an item in an array is always the number of items up to the item, minus one. For example, the first item in an array is at index zero, the second item in an array is at index one, the third is at index two and the fourth is at index three.

Looping through an iterator

A very common task for a software engineer is looping through an iterator (an object that you can traverse through all the values of). There are various loops, but by far, the most common is a for loop, which allows for initialization, maintenance and termination conditions. This allows outputting large amounts of data, manipulating data and performing repetitive tasks.

Let's say we only wanted the even numbers, in an array of ten numbers. We can loop through the array, add a condition to check if each number is even and only output these even numbers. This example demonstrates the usage of a for loop when filtering data.

Data types

A data type is a way of classifying data, so that the compiler knows how the data is independent to be used. The most commonly used data types are:

- Integer (1,2,3)
- String ("Anything inside quotation marks")
- Boolean (true or false)
- Floating point (12.3)
- Character (&#33)

Algorithms and big O notation

In computer science an algorithm is a series of steps for solving a problem. Algorithms take some input and produce some output for a computational problem. Most broadly, an algorithm is just a series of steps that perform a particular computation.

In the Python programming language there is a function called "max" which finds the largest item in a set of items. For example, if there are 5 numbers in a set, the max function would return the highest number.

There are various kinds of algorithms and when interviewing for companies it is likely you will be asked about them. However, it is rare for a software engineer to actually create an algorithm, it's more common to just copy an algorithm that's already been written. For more in depth information on algorithms and preparing for interviews, consider reading **Introduction to Algorithms**.

The Big O notation is used to describe how long an algorithm takes to run, more specifically, how long an algorithm takes to run relative to the input, in the worst-case scenario.

When using an algorithm to solve a problem, it's important for a software engineer to consider the performance of the algorithms given growing data as if it runs slowly, it will decrease the performance of the software.

The Big O notation uses mathematical functions to describe an algorithm's performance by putting the letter O in front of a time complexity (power or time computer needs to run the algorithm). For example, the best performing algorithms are constant time algorithms which are given the symbol "O(1)" which means these algorithms take the same time no matter the input size.

For more further information on the Big O notation, consider reading **Grokking Algorithms: An Illustrated Guide for Programmers and Other Curious People**.

The compiler

When running a program, most are unaware of what is actually going on, underneath the hood. A compiler is one such example, and is useful for a software engineer to understand. A compiler is a program that transforms high level programming languages to a low-level machine-readable language.

Some programmers write in high level programming languages include Python, Perl, PHP, ECMAScript, Ruby, C#, Java and many others however computers cannot read these types of languages. This is where the compiler converts the high-level programming language to machine readable code such as binary.

The compiler has a distinct advantage over other translation methods which is compilation, which is where the high-level programming language is converted into machine readable code in one go. Compilers have additional features, such as error checking which tells the user there are bugs in the code before running and optimization of code which runs code quicker and takes up less space.

The terminal

The terminal is a text-based system used to navigate the operating system and can be used to open, create, delete files and directories. Nowadays the terminal comes with shells which are programs that make it easier to navigate through your files. Popular shells include bash, zsh and power shell.

As a software engineer, there are terminal commands that you will use on a daily basis, so it's useful to get familiar with the most popular ones. Below are commands and examples of their usage (in italics) in Unix-like operating systems.

- cd (change directory): *cd "path/to/directory"*
- ls (list directory): *ls "path/to/directory"*
- open (open a file): *open "file name"*
- mkdir (make new directory): *mkdir directory_name*
- rm -r (remove a directory): *rm -r "path/to/directory"*
- sudo (executes command with superuser privilege): *sudo "command"*
- clear (clears terminal of all previous commands): *clear*
- whatis (get one line description of a command): *whatis "command"*
- exit (close terminal session): *exit*
- rmdir (removes empty directory): *rmdir "path/to/directory'*

Version control

Most software projects are updated on a daily basis and have multiple people contributing to them. If someone makes a change to the software project, the other people working on the project would need to have access to the changed version of the project to prevent their work conflicting. Also, if a mistake was made in the code, rolling back to a previously working version can be a nightmare without version control.

Version control, tracks every individual change and stores it, so if a mistake has been made, contributors can just roll back to a previous version. Also, it allows users to pull the latest version of the code, to prevent possible conflicts. The most popular version control tools are Git, SVN and CUS. Below are some of the most popular commands in Git along with examples of their usage (in italics).

Git Commands

- git init (initializes the current folder as git repository): *git init*

- git status (see which files are staged and tracked by git): *git status*

- git add (add files to staging area): *git add .*

- git commit (commit changes to the git repository): *git commit -m "insert name of commit"*

- git log (see log of commits and their id): *git log*

- git checkout (navigate between the branches created by git branch): *git checkout <name of branch>*

Online git repositories commands (GitHub)

- git remote add origin (add the remote online repository): *git remote add origin <repository url>*

- git push -u origin (push the local git repository contents to the online repository): *git push -u origin <branch name>*

- git clone (clone an online Git repository to your computer): *git clone <repository url>*

Maths for software engineers

There are some mathematical ideas that are useful for software engineers to understand. However, for the average programmer building applications in the business world, there isn't a requirement to be particularly good at mathematics, beyond a high school level.

There are sub sections of software development that do require a high level of mathematical knowledge such as in the financial or scientific industries. However, software development does require having a high level of aptitude in logic and problem solving which is also required in mathematics. Which is why the best programmers being often also great at maths.

There are certain mathematical topics that are more useful than others in software development. Understanding "discrete mathematics", which is the study of mathematical structure, will have more cross over to programming than calculus.

In general, most complicated mathematical formulae that you may need to use whilst programming, have already been built and can be accessed through libraries and pre-existing functions, so the need to recall and understand mathematical formulae is for the most part unnecessary.

Rather having an aptitude for building mental models will have a greater benefit in your journey as a software engineer. If you would like to learn more about mathematics in software development, consider reading **Concrete Mathematics: A Foundation for Computer Science**.

Object orientated design

Object oriented programming (OOP) is a programming paradigm that was created to deal with increasing complexity of large software systems. It is about representing things we see in the world using classes and objects. Whether working on the front-end or back-end you will encounter classes and objects.

Classes are like blueprints, recipes or schematics that show what every instance of the class should contain. While objects are created from classes. An object created from a class is called an instance. This prevents having to create the same object many times. Classes contain methods and attributes (like keys in dictionaries). Attributes are variables that hold data types whilst methods hold behaviour. There are four main concepts in OOP:

1. **Encapsulation**: The process of combining data and functions into a class. In encapsulation, data cannot be accessed directly. It's accessed through certain methods provided by the class.

2. **Polymorphism**: The ability for a method to have different behaviours for an inherited class.

3. **Inheritance**: Class inherits behaviour from another class, this allows the defining of basic classes with large reusability.

4. **Abstraction**: Show only the essential attributes to the user and hide unnecessary methods and attributes from the user.

The above OOP concepts are theoretical, and took me a while to implement but as a beginner useful to keep in mind whilst reading or creating classes and objects.

User interface and user experience

UI (user interface) and UX (user experience) are the visual aesthetics or layout of a page. A well-designed site, builds trust and helps users find what they are looking for. For websites and applications, UI/UX is a vital part of the development process, but sometimes overlooked.

Typically, the task of improving UI and UX is the responsibility of the UI/UX designer. But as a software engineer working on the front-end, having a basic understanding of general design principles will add another tool to your arsenal and allow you to build applications that increase customer satisfaction and ultimately increase the number of users. Outlined below are the general design principles to keep in mind when building customer facing applications.

Consistency

Being consistent in design, means keeping repeated elements on the web page looking and behaving in the same way. The two types of consistency to focus on:

1. Style Consistency

This means the below styles are consistent across all elements on the page.

- Typography
- Colour
- Hover effects
- Alignment
- Spacing

2.   Functional Consistency

Elements that look the same, should perform the same functionality. This makes the site more predictable and easier to use.

Hierarchy

Creating an order of importance for elements in order to focus the user's attention on the focal point of the page and make information easier to consume. This is done through the use of colour, contrast, texture, shape, positioning, orientation and size.

<u>White Space</u>

White space is the space between elements on a page, this could be the empty space between graphics, page margins, columns or lines. Adding the correct amount of white space, adds emphasis to important content, creates a balance and overall improves user experience. The amount of white space should reflect the pauses the visitor takes while reading. It's like visual breathing space for the eyes.

By taking into consideration the above design principles when building customer facing applications, it will help to improve user experience and customer satisfaction.

How the web works?

It is important to understand how the web browser works, as a software engineer, you will typically be building applications running on the web in one form or another. Simply put, when visiting a webpage using a computer or mobile, the client makes a request to the server (stores web page files), which sends the web pages to the client to display on the browser.

When a user types in an address for a webpage, the browser looks to the Domain Name Server (DNS) to find the IP address for the domain name you entered, so it can fetch the website files from the correct server. The DNS is like a phone book for websites.

If you go to **https://google.com** the browser will ask the DNS for the actual address which is "142.250.64.110" and the browser would send a request for the asset and code files from the server at that address.

Bits and bytes

A computer stores information at the smallest level in units, called bits which store either 0 or 1. A byte on the other hand is made up of 8 bits, and can store a single character e.g. "A". All storage in a computer is measured in bytes.

→

- **Kilobyte**, KB, about 1 thousand bytes
- **Megabyte**, MB, about 1 million bytes
- **Gigabyte**, GB, about 1 billion bytes
- **Terabyte**, TB, about 1 trillion bytes (rare)

Clean code

Writing clean code is fundamental when building software. Clean code can be understood as code that is:

- Easily understand
- Easily modifiable
- Easily tested
- Works correctly

Writing code that gets the job done requires a relatively low programming skill level. The higher skilled software engineers write clean code that can be easily understood by themselves and other software engineers.

Martin Fowler the author of **Refactoring: Improving the Design of Existing Code** says *"Any fool can write code that a computer can understand. Good programmers write code that humans can understand.".* Writing code that can be easily understood has multiple benefits:

- Easier to understand, thus easier to modify and add features.

- Long term, save on engineer's time as they will not need to spend time trying to understand the code.

- Reduced file sizes, because code will be able to be reused

- Scalability, if software will have a ten-year shelf life other engineers will likely join the team and will need to quickly understand the code base to work on it.

There are a multitude of concepts to understand, in order to write clean code and every company has their own conventions for writing clean code. Below are two concepts that are quite commonly discussed in software development and are often implemented in everyday code.

1. **Single Responsibility Principle**: Every module, class, function should only do one thing.

2. **Naming Convention**: As programmers, you will be naming lots of variables, methods, classes. Using intention meaning names that describe what they do and how they are used.

There are plenty of other clean code concepts that are useful to learn (I just included the two I think are the most common). For further reading on writing clean code, please view **Clean Code: A Handbook of Agile Software Craftsmanship**.

Software development methodologies

A development methodology regulates how tasks in a project are organized and carried out. The two most common software development methodologies are agile and waterfall. Both have their advantages and disadvantages, but currently agile is by the far the most popular methodology in software development with recent studies showing a majority of organizations preferring agile over waterfall [16].

The reason for agile popularity is the methodology offers responsiveness to changes in user requirements, which is useful to meet users evolving requirements.

The agile methodology is a process for a project which involves constant iteration and collaboration to meet more of the demands of the user. Within the agile methodology there are principles such as individuals and interactions over processes and tools, working software over comprehensive documentation and responding to change over following a plan.

The agile methodology embodies methods to promote the values of the methodology such as Extreme Programming, Scrum, Kanban, Lean, FDD (Feature-Driven Development), Crystal, DSDM (Dynamic Systems Development Method). One of the most popular methods is called "Scrum" which manages software development projects through a series of iterations called sprints.

Each sprint encompasses all phases of the software development model such as plan, design, build, testing and support. There have been plenty of books written on the agile methodology, but I would suggest **Doing Agile Right: Transformation Without Chaos**.

The waterfall software development methodology is less popular than agile and differently to agile, the software development model is conducted in non-repeatable linear phases. This means all the planning and designing needs to be done before any building and testing can take place.

The main problem with the waterfall methodology is it does not easily allow for change in requirements. This means all problems have to be foreseen in the planning phase of the software development lifecycle, which is hard to do (especially if the software is complicated).

Chapter 6: Soft skills For Software Engineers

"You can have brilliant ideas but if you can't get them across, your ideas won't get you anywhere" - Lee Iacocca

For most software engineers, *"developing software is easy, people are hard"*. Given enough time and resources most engineering problems can be solved, however people can be irrational and emotional which makes them difficult to "solve". Whether a software engineer likes it or not, effectively communicating with people is essential to maintaining and progressing in their career.

Soft skills are skills that enable you to communicate and interact with others. An individual with good softs skills typically has a higher than average EQ (emotional intelligence). They score high in empathy, communication, open mindedness, humility and confidence. Listed below are some common soft skills, which once you recognised, will enable you to develop these soft skills.

Empathy

One of the most important soft skills to have as a software engineer is empathy. This is being able to understand what the other person is experiencing from their point of view.

This is useful when communicating with people, because it allows you to predict how a person will react to what we say, allowing one to communicate with others at a deeper level. For example, if a person doesn't react well to criticism ensure positive communication towards him for higher levels of performance.

Being empathetic is also extremely useful during the coding process, as it allows you to view software from the perspective of others. This could mean being empathetic to other software engineers and yourself by writing documentation and using naming conventions so they are more easily able to read your code in the future. Also, empathy towards users of the software which results in creating a better product because you are able to put yourself in their shoes and as a result anticipate their needs.

Empathy allows us to see both sides of a technical debate. If we convey we understand both sides of a debate (known as the 'sandwich approach') it makes the other members in the debate feel validated and understood. This has the added benefit of being able to influence and effectively communicate with them in the future.

Accountability and humility

As a software engineer, it is inevitable that you will make mistakes during the course of your career. Some of these mistakes will not be noticed by others, whilst others could have a major impact on the business.

Either way, it is advisable to take ownership of these mistakes in order to learn and grow as a software engineer. This doesn't mean purposefully broadcasting every mistake you make, but taking an internal note of the mistake and seeking to investigate why it happened and what can be done to prevent it happening again. In some instances, it would be necessary to let others know of the mistake, especially if it affects the end user.

It is human nature to hide and cover up mistakes for fear of ruining their reputation. So, it's important that senior software engineers and leadership to foster a culture of positive accountability, which allows individuals to take ownership of their mistakes whilst not being punished.

Humility, as a software engineer, is also essential to progress in one's career. It's easy to fall into the trap of thinking you know better than others because you have a certain number of years of experience, a certain qualification or hold a certain position in the company.

However, other staff members who do not have those attributes, can also have valuable insights and by acknowledging their insights it's likely you will learn, improve team relations which will help you progress in your career.

Time management

Software engineers must be time-conscious, after almost all software engineers on for their time. Typically, the responsibility of managing a software engineer's time falls upon the project manager. But the engineers who manage their own time most efficiently are normally the ones that get the most done and as a result progress their career the furthest.

One way to do this is to give accurate time estimates for tasks as well as sticking to them. The junior level engineers tend to not stick to deadlines as much as senior engineers, this is just because senior engineers have more of a detailed understanding of each step that makes up a proposed task.

Another way software engineers manage their time is through prioritizing tasks according to their level of their importance. The level of importance is dependent on various factors such as goal, value and completion time for a particular task. Tasks can be prioritized a number of ways, such as the '**Eisenhower Matrix**' which is a framework used to help prioritize tasks according to importance and urgency.

Communication

A software engineer's job involves communicating within the software development team and typically across multiple different teams such as sales, customer support, product management, operations and much more. For this reason, communication is a key part of the job.

Software development processes already have built in communication steps for example daily stand up, design reviews, code reviews and documentation. One of the major differences between a junior and senior engineer or lead engineer, is their communication skills, as these roles often require leadership. So, becoming a strong communicator is essential for career progression.

There are a few strategies, a software engineer can implement to become a strong communicator. First, when communicating with non-technical team members about software, it's advisable to get into a habit of giving a high-level overview of software, rather than giving very specific detailed explanations.

For example, if a software engineer is asked to explain a feature it would be better to give a general overview of the feature using non-technical language than to give a detailed overview with all the technical jargon. This is because a non-technical person will not understand the technical details and as a result frustrate others and waste time.

Another strategy to improve communication is to have discussions in the open rather than in one-one conversations. By having discussions in the open, in front of individuals who are able to contribute to the discussion we improve the chances of having a better solution.

Teamwork and collaboration

Software development is a team game, even if you're the only engineer, it's most probable that you will work with project managers, designers, customer support and others. This means a software engineer must be able to work within a team in order to succeed.

Teamwork is the combined action of a group, with each individual doing their part, towards a common goal. As an individual this could mean helping the team achieve the goal by being reliable, collaborative, flexible and diligent. A software engineer can demonstrate this by helping others complete their tasks, mentoring other software engineers, meeting deadlines and being diligent about the code they produce.

Chapter 7: The paths of a software engineer

Be language agnostic. Language is just a tool. It's valuable to know a language deeply, but it's also valuable to be learning new things. The best engineers tend not to identify as a ____ engineer. - Gayle Laakmann McDowell

In software development, there are areas software engineers can specialize in. There are highly specialized areas such as DevOps and software testing which are highly paid, and then there are the major paths in software development.

The major paths we will be discussing in this chapter are; front-end development, backend development and full stack development. It is important to note that choosing a single software development path does not mean you will not have to learn topics in the other paths, there is plenty of crossover. In fact, as a software engineer it will be expected to have basic understanding and skills included in other paths.

For example, if you are a front-end engineer you would be expected to have a basic understanding of how the backend worked. With the creation of new languages and methodologies every year, the path to any of the software developments will change yearly, however there are some general requirements that have stayed the same which are included in the below sections.

Front-end engineer path

A front-end engineer is responsible for building the user interface and will create the code that will run inside the browser. A front-end engineer should at a minimum understand the topics mentioned in "Chapter 6: The self-taught software engineer coding roadmap" and at least be proficient in the following languages:

- HTML
- CSS
- CSS Framework e.g. SCSS
- Vanilla JavaScript

- One JavaScript framework e.g. React JS, Vue or Angular

Back-end engineer path

A backend engineer is responsible for building the server side of an application, for example building an API that front-end engineers can utilize. A back-end engineer should understand the topics mentioned in "Chapter 6: The self-taught software engineer coding roadmap" as well as be proficient in the following:

- One server-side programming language e.g. PHP, Python and Ruby
- SQL
- SQL dialect e.g. PostgreSQL, MySQL and Oracle

Full Stack engineer path

A full stack engineer is responsible for building the user interface and the server side of an application. This could be considered the hardest role as it requires being proficient at the languages mentioned for both front-end and back-end engineers.

Niche specialization

Once you've learnt the fundamentals of software development and have chosen what type of engineer you would like to be, the next step is to choose a framework language within that path. For example, if you choose backend development, choose one of the backend languages such as Ruby, Python and PHP.

Whilst some software engineers become proficient at many languages. In the beginning learning just one language will allow you to specialize and get that first software engineer job quicker. It is also important to become proficient at the language you chose, because the questions in the job interview will most likely revolve around the language you specialize in.

Within a particular software development language there are frameworks that one can specialize in. For example, currently within the Python language, the top three frameworks are; Django, Flask and Pyramid. By specializing in a particular language and framework, you will stand out to employers. It is possible to niche down further, by specializing in very specific areas such as database design, web animations or mobile development.

Before choosing the area to specialize in, it is wise to take into consideration which language, framework or skill has the most opportunities (use **Stackoverflow's annual survey**) and which you will enjoy using.

Mentorship

Learning a software development language to a proficient level, is a difficult task. For this reason, getting mentorship from a software engineer who has expertise in that language has a high return on investment. It will allow you to get answers to any problems you are stuck on and dramatically shorten your learning curve.

By spending time with an expert in the language, you can also pick up tips and tricks that you might not have learnt before. My personal experience with mentorship was with an online tutor who helped me understand some concepts I did not understand in Ruby on Rails.

Alternative career paths

Software engineers can do other jobs besides writing software. These roles could be for individuals who enjoy technology but are not riveted by the idea of coding all day. Or, if they want to get that first job as a software engineer, and use an alternative path to get their foot in the door.

Developer relations

Some software engineers are not excited about writing code all day and realize they prefer a career path which involves more interaction with others. One such career path is a developer relations role which involves building relationships with users and customers. This typically involves networking, speaking at conferences and managing social media accounts.

Sales Engineers

Another alternative career path is a sales engineer which involves establishing new and maintaining relationships with clients as well as persuading clients to purchase products and services. This position is rather unique as it requires a degree of technical knowledge, the ability to communicate this technical knowledge effectively as well as sales skills.

Technical Recruiter

A career as a technical recruiter offers an opportunity to connect and maintain relationships with others. It involves pairing software developers with companies that would be a good fit for each other. Unfortunately, recruiters often have a bad reputation, however if you already have a background in software development it will make recruiting a lot easier, as you will have more empathy and credibility than other recruiters.

Project Manager

Another career path commonly utilized by software engineers who no longer enjoy coding full time, is a role as a project manager. This involves establishing tasks and resources for the individuals working on the project, motivating and managing expectations of others. Understanding the requirements of the business and people skills are an essential part of the project manager role.

Chapter 8: Landing your first software engineering job

"Give me six hours to chop down a tree and I will spend the first four sharpening the axe." - Abraham Lincoln

Having personally gone through the experience of knowing nothing about software development to now having worked as a software engineer professionally for nearly two years, I have a reasonable idea of the steps needed to secure your first software engineer role.

In hindsight I would have done many things differently which would have reduced the time it took to land my first job in software development. In this chapter, we will go through various actions you can take to increase the chances of landing your first job in software development and prevent making common newbie mistakes when applying for roles.

Asking the right questions

If you've read up to this point in the book, ideally you should know which path of software development you would like to go down. Now before applying for a role, it is useful to identify exactly what kind of role you would like to work in. This can be done by answering the following questions:

1. What kind of industry do you want to work in?
2. Would you like to work remotely, in house or a combination of the two?
3. What size company do you want to work in?

By identifying exactly what kind of job you would like, you won't waste your time on jobs that don't meet your requirements which will increase the likelihood of landing the job you actually want. As someone who is looking to break into the industry and land their first role as a software engineer, it could be argued that you should take whatever software job you can get.

However, applying for software roles that you actually want has a higher success rate than applying for just any role. This is because your enthusiasm for the roles you want, comes through in the interview stage. Also applying for lots of roles can make one jaded and burnt out from the job application process.

Programming skills

Before even considering applying for a software engineer job, it is vital you are proficient in the languages, frameworks and skills for your chosen path (see Chapter 6: Software development paths). By applying for roles without the necessary skills you are unlikely to be successful in securing a software engineer role. And if you are successful, it is unlikely you will stay at that role for long.

There is a lot of debate about what makes a software engineer proficient in a software language. Some argue, being proficient in a software language is the ability to build applications from scratch without having to look at much reference material.

Once proficient in the languages needed in your software engineer path, having a solid portfolio of software development work is what will initially demonstrate your coding proficiency to employers.

Create a meaningful portfolio

A software developer portfolio is a collection of completed work, typically used to demonstrate a job applicant's competency. Nowadays portfolios are displayed on a website and include the following:

- Intended job title
- Specialized skills and software languages
- Short biography
- Years of experience
- Professional and personal accomplishments
- Portfolio projects

When creating portfolio projects, it is well worth having projects that were built using the languages you chose in Chapter 7: Software development paths. There should be at a minimum six projects, as this will enable you to demonstrate your speciality in your chosen languages.

Before building these projects it's useful to know what kind of jobs you want to apply for and tailoring your projects to those jobs. For example, if you would like to work in the financial technology industry it would be advisable to have portfolio projects related to financial technology.

When creating a portfolio, it's advisable to attach links to the GitHub repository and links to the actual project itself. This adds credibility to the project and allows potential employers to review the code that you have written. Providing a screenshots, title and short description of the project is also a nice touch.

Building a personal brand

Building a personal brand around software development demonstrates your passion and can increase the likelihood of landing that first software development job. This is because companies typically research candidates and if they find content demonstrating your enthusiasm for coding, it will make you stand out from other candidates.

With my own YouTube channel, I have been given numerous software development opportunities. Some ways to build a personal brand include:

- Blogging about your journey in software development
- Contributing to open source programming
- Regularly contribute to your GitHub
- YouTube channel with coding tutorials

Having a personal brand is not only useful for landing a job, but can provide an opportunity to make an additional income stream. It's also a great way to log your personal journey in software development.

Companies to avoid working for

When a company is looking to hire software engineers, they will put a process in place to remove applicants that they believe are not a good fit. This process is put in place to prevent applicants that may reduce productivity whilst working for their company. Similarly, applicants applying for roles should put a process in place to prevent working for companies that will reduce their productivity.

The process of vetting companies depends on the applicant's requirements, however there are companies, most applicants would not like to work for. These companies have toxic work environments where employees are unhappy and overworked.

Typically, these companies look for applicants who are looking to break into the industry. Having experienced applying and working for companies like this, there are red-flags to watch out for during the application process:

- The job description mentions doing tasks outside the normal tasks of a software engineer.
- Employee turnover rate is high.
- The company is not willing to invest in your growth.
- The salary is much lower than the average salary for such a position.
- There are no other technical staff members.

- Working overtime and weekends is expected.

- They do not have a software development team (you will be the only developer)

While this is not a definitive list, by using the list as an indicator you will be well positioned to avoid the companies that will not help you develop as a software engineer.

Create a meaningful CV

An important part of an application for a software engineer job, is the CV. Typically the CV and cover letter will be viewed by a CV screener who has a checklist of requirements and only if those requirements are met will you be put forward for the next stage. For software engineers a CV is meant to demonstrate software languages you specialize in, years of experience, education history, working history, skills and portfolio projects.

There are plenty of guides on the do's and don'ts when creating a software development CVs, one I found particularly useful was **A Good Tech Resume**.

A useful takeaway from this guide for self-taught software engineers applying for their first role is to create a version of the resume for that specific job description. This involves re-editing your resume so it is similar to the language used in the job description. This moves your CV from being generic to being more specific for the role which will undoubtedly make it stand out.

With so many applications for engineer roles, standing out is not an easy task. Typically, recruiters spend less than six seconds scanning a CV, before deciding to reject or move the applicant onto the next stage.

One way to stand out is to create a mini introductory video, explaining who you are and the role you are applying for. By doing this, the CV screener gets an idea of what kind of person you are and we have found an increased response rate. Some self-taught software engineers have found adding the company logo as a background image on the video is a nice personal touch and further increases the response rate from CV screeners.

Sending applications

Choosing your niche and specializing is a great way to stand out to employers. If you have specialized it's also important you market yourself as a specialist. This can be done by including the language, framework or skill you have specialized within your title, for example:

- Python Django engineer (specializing in design systems)
- React JS engineer (specializing in animations)
- Ruby on Rails engineer
- PHP Laravel engineer

By specializing you also reduce the pool of companies you can apply for, which will have the added benefit of making the sending application process easier. When sending applications, it has been useful for me to split the process in two stages.

1. Identifying potential employer:

a.   Searching for jobs with your specialization e.g. PHP Laravel engineer or even finding companies who use your particular specialization e.g. Airbnb uses Ruby on Rails.

b.   Check if they will be a good fit for your requirements as mentioned in asking the right questions section.

2.   Sending applications:

a.   Once you've identified a company you feel will be a good fit, send in your CV, cover letter and a video introduction. If the company doesn't seem to be actively hiring, still apply because there is always the chance they are still looking.

b.   Sending as many job applications to employers who fit your requirement will undoubtedly increase the chances of landing your first role. I have found having a goal of sending out a new application on a daily basis to be the most fruitful.

Sending out as many applications as possible to companies you want to work for, increases the likelihood of landing interviews.

Dealing with job recruiters

As a software engineer, although you can earn a pretty penny from freelancing, it is still advised to get a nine-to-five job. Not only does a stable job provide you with a routine, it also allows you to progress up the corporate ladder in more than one direction. Remember, each form of passive income coupled with a stable job provides more opportunities for skill growth and personal or professional development.

So, when you start looking for a job, you will most likely focus on recruiters. These recruiters will either headhunt you or have an accessible online portal where you can submit your curriculum vitae (CV). The main question many on this path have is concerning what recruiters actually look for when hiring a software engineer.

The answer is not as simple as "getting noticed" but instead focuses more on how you get the recruiters to notice you. Naturally, this would mean that you need to be active in the developer ecosystem. But where exactly are these spaces that have these recruiters scourging for talent? Surprisingly, Twitter is one of the go-to spaces recruiters will visit.

Typically, Twitter is viewed as a spot for internet gossip about the new celebrity relationships; however, it also allows you to not only identify but also interact with others in your field. There are so many software development gurus on Twitter, and by staying updated with their works, you are pivoting your mindset toward learning what is current within your field. Not to mention, new and ground-breaking tech information are fantastic conversation starters, especially when delving into the recruitment process.

LinkedIn is a fantastic network that will not only allow you to join programming and developer groups, but also scout out and apply for opportunities that companies may list on their LinkedIn pages. This is why it is important to remain active on your page. Studies show that to increase your chances of finding a job on LinkedIn, you should try to post something within your field's context every three to four days. You could even link your online portfolio and GitHub to LinkedIn posts just to show recruiters what you are capable of.

Once you have caught the eye of a recruiter, they will pool more candidates together before starting to filter them. There are three main criteria that will be used to filter candidates. These are as follows: educational background, work history, and tech stack match.

The most confusing of the three will most likely be the last. Remember that technologically-focused companies will most likely look for individuals who are familiar with their dominant language of code, operational procedures, and the theory behind how to link the two together. When starting off, you may want to target small businesses and start-ups, which will definitely focus on a potential software engineer who can adapt quickly.

When you make it past the screening call and into the interview phase, it is time to shine! It's here you can, show your level of interest in building software. Focus on how this new work venture will fit in with your career's trajectory. Try to factor in how the company could use your skills at this time.

Keep in mind that each workplace is unique, which is why you want to show cultural sensitivity and mention core values during your interview. For example, a recruiter may focus on clean code, punctuality, and respect. At this point, it is all about giving the recruiter what they want, seeing as you have already proven your skill set as a software engineer.

Acknowledge your weaknesses. Also, tell them that you will lean on others for assistance when needed and you will maintain professional levels of respect and integrity. Follow the above steps, and you are guaranteed to impress any recruiter that comes across your path. Don't forget—recruiters talk. One opportunity may just lead to another and with better prospects, too.

Interviews

If you keep sending out applications, you will eventually get past the CV screening phase and the potential employees will request an interview. The type of interview you experience will vary, however normally the first interview is informal and is where the employer checks if you would be a culture fit for the company. Passing this type of interview depends largely on social skills, and this is an area in my experience, software engineers are often lacking. However here are a few useful tips to prepare you for these kind of interviews:

- Research the company and prepare a few bullet points to demonstrate you have researched them.

- Try not to interrupt the interviewee when they are speaking.

- Use language the interviewee is using, this makes the person feel like you have listened to what they have said.

- Aim to be clear and concise. Waffling will cause the interviewee to get tired and want to end the interview.

- If you do not know an answer to a question, attempt to answer it and if you cannot mention you will get back to them with an answer at a later date. This will demonstrate persistence to the employer.

- If a non-technical person is the interviewee do not use technical jargon or language they would not understand.

- Prepare a few questions about the role to ask at the end of the interview.

The informal interview is mostly there to check if you are a cultural fit. Which in simple terms means, checking if you are a normal person. To prepare for culture fit questions, it would be wise to research the company's culture. To give you an idea below are five software engineer culture fit questions:

- Describe a work environment in which you felt most productive and happy?
- Have you had a best friend at work? What do you think about becoming friends with your co-worker's?
- When working with others, describe your preferred relationship with them.
- What is your preferred work style? Do you prefer working in a team or alone?
- Can you tell me about a problem you found difficult to solve and how did you end up solving it?

Once you pass this, you will typically be moved onto the technical interview which is where the interviewer (most likely a software engineer) will ask technical questions to assess your aptitude. The technical questions will revolve around the programming languages you have learnt and possibly software development methodologies and concepts (mentioned in Chapter 6). Below I've included some questions that were asked during interviews I have partaken in:

- Can you briefly explain the S-O-L-I-D principles?
- In JavaScript, what is a prototype?
- Can you explain why writing tests is important in software development?

Once you're finished with the technical interview, the interviewer will often say they will get back to you, with the result soon. If you are unsuccessful, it is common for companies to not let you know that you have been unsuccessful.

For this reason, I would recommend asking the company for a time frame, by which they should let you know the result of the interview. By doing this, you prevent the stress of wondering whether you passed or not. Lastly, asking for feedback at the end of the interview is a great way to figure out your blind spots so you can improve for the next interview.

The technical interview phase is the hardest and is the phase where most candidates are rejected. Also depending on the company, there could be multiple technical interviews. This is because companies pay software engineers for the most part on their technical abilities, so applicants who are not up to the standard are removed.

The technical interview phase can also include take home projects. The take home test is where the company provides a technical test or project to be completed outside the actual interview.

Once completed the applicant will send the test to the company who will assess whether it is up to the required standard. In my experience taking home projects are time consuming so I'd suggest asking the company to pay for the time you worked on the project or at the very least they guarantee providing feedback.

Negotiating job offers

If you pass the technical interview, you will be made an offer. This is where the company provides the salary and possible benefits they provide in exchange for your services as a software engineer. From the start of the interview process the company will be trying to gage the type of benefits and salary you require.

The interviewer will ask questions such as, "What kind of salary and benefits do you want?". By answering this question directly, you will most likely lowball the amount and possibly lose out on a lot of money. For this reason, it's best to avoid this salary question. However, this can prove tricky in an interview situation. The below steps will give you a guideline on how to avoid the salary question:

1. Politely refuse to answer the question e.g. *"It's a little too early in the process to discuss salary"*.

2. Maybe the reason they asked this salary question, is they are worried you are out of their price range so address their concerns e.g.

"I'm sure that we will be able to come to an agreement on salary late on in the process"

3. Return the question so you can get an estimate of the type of price range they are offering e.g. *"Can you tell me more about the price range you had in mind?"*

If you are successful in retrieving the range of salary the company is willing to offer, then you might be able to get a higher salary than you wished for. Even if they make a great offer, it's always negotiate the offer. You can read more about the reasons for this in an article written by a former poker player turned Airbnb software engineer called **The Ten Rules for Negotiating a Job**.

Most companies secretly respect candidates who negotiate, because it shows competency and indicates you have options. The top candidates always negotiate because they have options. There are also employee benefits that can be negotiated and enquired about such as:

*   PTO or vacation days
*   Tuition reimbursement/education incentives

- Stock options

- Option to work remotely

- 401K or pension schemes

- Personal and family leave

- Relocation assistance

- Sick time

- Health club memberships

Once you've negotiated and accepted the offer, you can celebrate knowing you've landed your first job developing software. In the next chapter we will go through some insider secrets that will help you whilst you work as a software engineer.

Chapter 9: Working as a software engineer

"Truth can only be found in one place: the code." -
Robert C. Martin

A day in the life of a software engineer

The day of a software engineer can start at different
times, which is also one of the many perks of the job.
What some software engineers do is schedule their
meetings with co-workers and clients for the morning,
giving them time during the day to work on intensive
tasks, refine discussed content, and get a chance to go
over the topics of that evening.

The customers who software engineers interact with
most likely demand prompt delivery of their projects,
which you may want to ensure happens. A happy
customer means a happy employee. It is very
important to make sure that you are always up-to-date
with what your customer requirements are.

Teamwork makes the dream work

Working as a software engineer is not easy. On any given day, your customer will have one idea, and on the next day, they may have come up with another idea that supersedes their previous one. This can be extremely time-consuming. To avoid too drastic of a change, try to ensure that the customer receives constant feedback from you.

This is why it's important to stay on the same page, especially when you're involved in an agile project. Remember, when you are doing a brainstorming sprint, you want the entire team to be aware of what's going on, and you also want the customer to be involved as much as possible.

With that being said, your team remains a core component of the project's outcome. Team members don't just want to work; they want to feel valued. Therefore, as a software engineer, take some time to get to know your crew. Whether it's bonding over a beer or discussing video games during a lunch break, team dynamics will influence the amount and quality of work that is produced.

Keep the meetings as full of life as possible. How many teams tackle this is by letting each member have a chance to lead the team meeting. Not only does this force every person to know what is going on with the project, but it also allows a constant interaction within the team. It is through this route that software engineers are the most proficient and efficient.

You have probably heard the saying "teamwork makes the dream work". Well, you wouldn't be wrong to agree with it, seeing as teamwork has proven to encourage creativity, improve the skills of all involved, and boost personal morale. As a software engineer, you want to ensure that the customer's time to market is achieved as quickly as possible without compromising on the quality of the end product.

By evoking a strong sense of community within your team, focusing on improving them mentally, emotionally, and even physically, you will increase the chance of success as a software engineer.

A point of contention, especially when starting your journey as a software engineer, is getting along with your co-workers. Keep in mind that a toxic work environment will not create a great end product. With that being said, below are a few ways to get along with your colleagues.

An important aspect to remember is that you do not have to be friends with all of your colleagues. However, this does not mean that you should not respect them. This can be done in so many different ways, ranging from giving credit for others work someone else has done to offering tea or coffee if you are going to be making some. Respect can go a very long way, even if you need someone's assistance in the future.

Avoid cringe-worthy topics that are deemed inappropriate in the office environment. For example, suddenly bringing up religion, politics, and a co-worker's sex life will not make you liked by others.

Don't forget to put yourself in their shoes. Would you feel comfortable answering questions regarding these topics, especially when in a room full of co-workers? You do not want to be known as that guy that asked about another's sex life. Leave this type of banter out of the workplace, ensuring that the topics that are discussed, if personal, remain professional.

Be sure that you're practicing appropriate office etiquette whenever possible. Having good manners will help to further your career as a software engineer. Try your best to avoid distracting others from their work. Resist posting that funny joke on the workplace's group chat during office hours, and ensure that you are mindful of the thoughts, ideas, and shared experiences that your co-workers provide during a conversation.

Do not partake in gossip. It is one of the quickest ways to get on the wrong side of co-workers, as well as to expose your true intentions as a professional. Although you may find gossip a point of discussion with others, adding fuel to the fire will only make you seem untrustworthy to the team. Co-workers will feel that they cannot share any information with you, which may even make you become isolated.

As a software engineer, you are bound to make mistakes. This is all a part of the learning process. Nobody becomes a software engineer and automatically knows everything. With that being said, you need to be honest about when you make an error.

Shifting the blame onto other co-workers will make them dislike you very fast, and it will cause an even greater detriment to you in the long-run. Being able to acknowledge your own faults and shortcomings is the first step in being able to effectively overcome them in the future.

As a software engineer, there will be a multitude of opportunities to prove your respect to the team. However, the ease at which this is done can only be fully understood once you have dealt with any lingering office politics that are present. As a software engineer, you are most likely going to interact with a number of employees on a daily basis, each with a different role to play in bringing the customer's ideas to fruition. With this large team comes many opinions, personal lives, and varying degrees of work ethic, which should be respected.

Office politics

Depending on the size of the company you are working for, the impact that office politics will have on the end product will increase exponentially. In small companies, new ideas are accepted quickly and actions are initiated faster. This is, however, not the same in big companies where, as the software engineer, you will have more individuals contesting you on your ideas.

An add-on to this is the degree of agreement that is required when a new decision is being made based on customer feedback. More individuals will need to accept the changes in a big company compared to a smaller company. As a software engineer, this can seem rather tedious, especially since you want to get the ball rolling on the project that lies ahead. However, this is unfortunately the way of the working world, which you will adapt to, the more you immerse yourself in large corporate working environments.

Code reviews

As a software engineer, you will be plagued by code reviews, especially seeing as they will improve your code quality as well as have a heightened benefit on not only the company's culture, but also the team dynamics.

For those of you who do not know what a code review is, it is essentially a form of peer review for those within the tech space. When one performs a code review, it is with the main intent of sharing knowledge, ensuring that there is both consistency in the completed code as well as the rectification of any accidental errors that may have been missed during the first revision process. It is by no means a malicious intent toward a software engineer, but more so a way to identify key and recurring problems that can be immediately addressed.

When you conduct a code review, depending on the team you are a part of, there may be different approaches to this process. Some teams may focus on reviewing all of the changes that are about to be merged into the main branch, whereas other teams might want a full and concise run-through of the entire project's code. The establishment of a code review institutes a collaborative environment where individuals can learn from each other's unique approaches toward conducting a code review.

Another question that has no definitive answer is, "When should I conduct a code review?" Again, it will depend on the nature of the team you are working with. Many teams prefer to perform a code review when the automated checks have been completed, whilst others prefer to perform a code review both before and after the automated check. One of the most utilized "when to review" strategies adopted is performing the code review before the code is to be merged to the mainline branch of the repository.

Remember that your code review will most likely be reviewed by someone else. This means that you need to ensure that a self-reviewed, complete, and self-tested code review is submitted. This also means that you need to allow enough time for your code review to be checked effectively. Usually, smaller chunks of reviewed codes are preferred, as this will track initial changes that could cause major end user fallout later down the production line.

Now that you have some more insight into the day and life of a software engineer, you can probably see that it is not the easiest career path to follow. However, the benefit is clear, especially as you start to organize your work around your life and not the other way around. Being a software engineer is rewarding work. This is even truer once you start to develop your interpersonal skills while also aiding those with a vision to change the world the opportunity to do so.

The end user is king

The thrill of getting a new project is one that few feelings compare to. Your excitement heightens as you allow your innovation to run wild, thinking of the best possible way to bring your customer's work to life. However, you need to remember that this is not your project, even though, as a software engineer, you are bringing it to life.

This is where we need to constantly question our approach to new tasks within the project's spectrum. We need to ask ourselves, "Is what I am doing bringing out the narrative that the customer wanted, or am I pouring too much of what I want/would change into their project?"

This is when we answer with the customer's end user in mind. In a way, you are the middleman, taking the information from one person to provide an outcome that benefits another group of individuals. The saying "the customer is always right" needs to be adapted to if it is going to fit the technological context.

Logically, the customer is not always right, especially if they act tech-savvy with no credentials to back up what they are saying.

However, as a software engineer, we need to think practically. The only method by which you are going to get the software you create to have the greatest reach is to pay attention to your customer. After all, they know the key end user better than you do, despite how much you believe you know about the project.

One of the most common mistakes that software engineers make, especially when they are at the early stages of their career, is believing that the end user is just like them.

We hate to break it to you, but the small yet significant group of tech-savvy individuals who you know are most likely not the end user your customer has in mind. Go into a project with an open mind and question all that you do, ensuring that you do not develop a restrictive approach towards the project.

Another common mistake many software engineers make is taking the path of least resistance, even if it is detrimental to the end user. As a software engineer, you need to take pride in your work, as any distaste toward the project will show in the result and negatively impact the end user.

How to really understand the environment and perspectives of the customer's end user is to literally walk a mile in their shoes. Engage your customer with eagerness, and ask them to describe a typical end user of their product.

If the end user is a fisherman, go on a fishing trip with some friends or family. Not only will this get you outside and into nature, but it will also foster a deep sense of inspiration in you that will only augment your path toward the project's completion.

Take your lived experience, and use it to conduct some key research. Find out how the end users feel, how they think, and what they say (or have said) in response to the idea that you are bringing to life.

You have the potential to change the lives of so many end users, having a knock-on effect on the worldwide economy, growth structures, and overall operations. Remember that your skill set can change the world, and you are the vessel that has been enlisted to do just that!

Chapter 10: Progressing in your career as a software engineer

"Simplicity is prerequisite for reliability" - *Edsger W.Dijkstra*

The field of software engineering is quickly becoming a competitive one. Opportunities are often given to those who are the most qualified. What this means is that if you are planning to move into a purely entrepreneurial direction with your skill sets, you will need to show that you know more, can do more, and can deliver more than your competition.

There are quite a few ways that this can be done; however, education is the greatest leveller. The more languages, experience and certification that you've added to your resume, and the work experience that you have obtained in an internship or job in a start-up or enterprise will only help propel you up to the next step on the corporate ladder.

Lifelong learning

The realm of software engineering is as dynamic as they come, with you not needing an office or designated workplace to become successful. With this, it means that your access to the current trends remains at your fingertips. But why would you need to remain up-to-date? To be completely honest, one doesn't have to constantly remain updated. However, it will definitely yield more benefits than if you chose to remain stagnant in your current knowledge base. In order to be successful as a software engineer, you need to remain relevant within the current job market.

For example, the future of coding would lead closer to new coding languages such as Swift, developed in 2014, than that of the C coding language that was developed in 1972. The more you're able to interact with current trends, the broader your business prospects will become. The broader your business prospects, the greater the number of opportunities you will have to grow as a software engineer. Become comfortable in being a life-long learner, as the opportunity to learn the next best coding system will always be readily accessible.

To progress up the ranks as a software engineer, you need to err on the side of productivity. You must think about how you can make technology better than what it already is. Creating solutions or modifying existing ones to problems that the masses face will ensure speedy uptake as well as provide you with the confidence to continue developing your chosen project. However, it is important that at this point one is not driven to burnout.

To grow and excel as a software engineer, you need to put in the hours. However, this should not be to the detriment of your mental health and the negative impact that your work may have on your friendships and relationships with your family. There are a few methods for remaining in the loop, and some of them might surprise you.

Although a lot of pictures about cats and dark humour can be found on Reddit, it definitely does provide a deep and current source of technological trends for software engineers. By viewing the sub-reddits of /r/programming, /r/webdev, and /r/(insert new code script), you are more than likely to find updates and tips on how to progress through your chosen code script with ease and effectiveness.

One of the largest tech start up hubs in the world is YCombinator. With this comes a smorgasbord of information that provides endless thought processes toward solving problems, along with the elaborate possibilities to grow your skill set. YCombinator's information page, including their news articles, are updated every week. So, ensure that you check back regularly.

Many discounts the power that podcasts have within the tech community. There are a multitude of different podcast producers out there, focusing on different aspects of software engineering, UX development, and product design.

You will find that many of these podcasts do not only focus on growing your trade, but also provide insight on how to grow yourself in both a personal and professional capacity [17]. For example, the Jeff Meyersonare podcast is a perfect starting channel in order to dip your toe into the world of podcasts. They also do not use too much jargon, which makes it perfect for those who are at the beginning or intermediary phases of growing as a software engineer.

Although it is important that we remain up-to-date with the new and the interesting, we cannot remain transfixed on them. Being a well-rounded software engineer is key. This means that you need to be well-versed in both the new and the current.

Focusing on the future trades and coding scripts will leave you never perfecting a single trade, decreasing your overall proficiency level as a software engineer. The sweet spot is the balance between honing your current market's trade and being inquisitive enough to identify the code and customer opportunities.

The art of networking

Software engineers need to be avid networkers. After all, one of the easiest ways to learn about new opportunities is to speak with those who offer them or know of someone else who does. As a software developer, you will most likely meet others at presentations, conferences, and hackathons. There are a few extra tips that you can utilize in order to ensure that you are making the most of all your networking opportunities.

An example of this is when you attend a presentation. Try to get to the presentation venue early, and ensure that you stay a little bit after it has concluded. Who knows, you may meet a talent scout who is looking for someone with your exact qualifications. You want to introduce yourself as quickly as possible, though not in a way that makes it seem as if you want something.

What many software developers do, especially when interacting with someone new, is ask them, "What software stack are you currently working in?" This shows that you are interested in their work and not just what they have to offer.

Networking is all about maintaining the connections right after the intended conference or presentation has concluded. This is why it is always advised to keep some business cards with you at all times. You don't necessarily need to own a business to have a business card, but just a card that has all of your core contact details on it.

Remember, asking for a business card is one of the easiest ways to finish a conversation, especially if you still plan on undertaking extensive networking opportunities at the same event [18]. With this being said, not all conversations will yield good networking opportunities. This is when you need to know which conversations are worth your time and which are not. However, the hard part is leaving these conversations without being tagged as rude.

Asking for a pay increase

Progressing up the hierarchical ladder as a software engineer may require you to be good at what you do as well as selling yourself. Remember that asking for a pay raise or promotion requires you to convince your employer that you are deserving of it. You want them to see that you are of more worth to the company than the typical 3% wage increase that occurs annually. This means that you want to ask your employer for a specific raise in pay, backing it up by making a list of goals and accomplishments while you have been with this specific company.

You should time this correctly. Catching your employer to talk about your pay raise right before his most important meeting of the day would yield poorer results than if you were to present your case ten minutes after your employer has arrived at the office.

Creating passive income sources

Starting out as a software engineer can be taxing in more ways than one, especially within the financial domain, as you never know when you are going to be fired. This is why it is recommended that a side hustle be adopted, this is to ensure that there is a stream of passive income. As a software engineer, a multitude of possibilities exist for you to use your skill sets to create an extra bit of cash.

Freelancing is a fantastic method for establishing a passive stream of income, particularly for those software engineers who have a little bit of extra time. However, one of the pitfalls is that you need to remain self-regulated, establishing enough time to successfully complete what is required from you in your day job. Platforms like Up work or Fiverr provide such a smorgasbord of opportunities that you can charge as much as you feel necessary for the skills required by others.

It is important to start by creating a name for yourself and not offering too high of a price for the services you offer. Once you start becoming a level one or two sellers, you can start to increase your prices as you see fit. You want to ensure that you create a large enough portfolio that you're able to show the extent of your talents. Once people can see that your services are well-received and rated highly, you will start to get an even larger customer bank.

A less common method of establishing a passive stream of income is through bug bounty hunting, which involves looking for any vulnerabilities that may be present in software, web-based applications, and websites. Many companies will use a method known as "crowdsourcing". This is where a lot of software engineer talents are sourced and hired to look for any bugs in the system.

If you have built your professional brand sufficiently, you will find that private corporations may headhunt you solely to validate and identify bugs within their projects. Looking at HackerOne and Bugcrowd are good first steps in becoming the next big bug bounty hunter [19].

Climbing the career ladder

Generally getting promoted varies between different companies but there are some general principles that will help software engineers climb the career ladder whatever company you are working for.

To continuously progress up a career ladder, you will need to be excellent what you do, this is especially the case as a software engineer. For software engineers this generally requires studying materials and coding outside of working hours. By improving your abilities, you will be able to help solve software problems for your team, which if done consistently will allow progression to a senior engineer position and beyond.

Progressing from a junior software engineer to a senior software engineer involves looking at a problem more broadly. When presented with a problem and possible solutions a junior engineer will typically take one of the solutions that have been presented.

The senior understands the customers problem and the code involved more deeply and will come up with alternative solutions, which could save time and prevent technical debt. The senior engineer, works at a different layer of abstraction as compared with the junior engineer and will often ask questions to understand the context further.

One technique to level up your coding skills and progress to a senior developer is through pair programming, which involves two software engineers, typically one senior and one junior coding on a single computer. The junior gets to pick the brain of the senior engineer and the senior gets to practice his teaching skills.

To become a senior engineer, being an excellent coder is not enough. There are soft skills, which senior engineers must have, because most likely, senior engineers will be managing junior engineers.

One of the most essential soft skills for a senior engineer is communication, this includes both oral and written. Half of a senior engineer's time will be dedicated to defining tasks to be implemented by others, technical management, supervision, relationship building and mentoring.

Some senior software engineers decide to progress to a project manager position. This involves a major mindset change, as the primarily role of this position is to create a path for the other project team members to achieve success where as a software engineer's role is primarily to make themselves achieve success.

Further up the career ladder are executive positions such as chief technology officer and technical director positions who are responsible for the management of an organization. These roles involve putting systems in place to meet the short term and long terms needs of the organization. Whilst these executive roles are paid extremely well, they are known for being stressful and getting into these positions is often dependent on making friends with the right people.

Becoming a Mentor

With the demand for software engineers increasing exponentially, there are more and more individuals who are interested in the career path. This provides a fantastic avenue to generate some passive income by becoming an online instructor. You can either create a course and upload it to an online marketplace, or if you have access to content platforms, you can market your course to those you know. Try taking a look at websites like BitDegree, Pluralsight, and Udacity to see how to navigate the course hosting platforms to see what's required to get started.

As you progress in your journey as a software engineer, you will find that there are many juniors who require guidance with regards to understanding the jargon used, why code needs to be written a specific way, and how to test whether your code is incorrectly written. One of the best ways to train and pass on your experiences is by talking through the coding processes when you are coding with them.

Remember, you were once a junior developer too who may or may not have required the experiential input from someone with more experience. Let the juniors explain their thoughts completely before correcting them. Interrupting them mid-sentence will not allow a change in their thought processes, which is what a mentor strives to impart on their mentee.

Ageism

Many believe that there is an inexplicable age limit that software engineers face. According to

SearchSoftwareQuality, 61% of software engineers who are older than 45 are concerned about their work prospects within their next 10 years in the software development industry [20]. However, the real question is this: With technology being future-focused, why are older software engineers seen as outcasts?

The answer is that many different employers assume that experience implies a stagnated skillset. This cannot be further from the truth, though, seeing as older software engineers know exactly where to look for updated information. Thus, although ageism is seen as a point of contention in the realm of software engineering, if you are able to prove your skills, no matter what your age, you should be allowed the opportunity to work in the field.

Chapter 11: Being Fulfilled and Happy as a Software Engineer

"A clever person solves a problem. A wise person avoids it." - *Albert Einstein*

Staying happy and fulfilled

Being a software engineer is a fulfilling career. Many people have dreamed of making a website, blog, or even mobile application. It is software engineers who take the vision that these individuals have and transform it into a reality! However, how can we expect a software engineer to operate at their best when mentally and emotionally they are struggling?

The emotional states that we find ourselves in play a critical role in how we perform our daily functions. There is a direct impact on the proficiency of our work. When we are happy, sad, or even angry, it will translate into the end product. However, logic prevails in this situation. If your mind is saturated with the dispute you had with your significant other that morning, you may experience hindered concentration levels at work.

Although there are some studies which assert that negative emotions can result in heightened analytical thinking due to constant questioning of the status quo, there is more research against that theory than for it.

To really understand what can cause a negative emotion to transpire in a software engineer, we need to look at the roles that they play within their work domain. A software engineer may find that they are doing the same job every single day with an overwhelming air of repetition. This lack of new opportunities hinders their innovative and creative thought processes, nullifying their abilities to think out of the box. This creates a declining loop of low motivation followed by a slower rate of coding and a stronger need to decline new opportunities because they feel unequipped and inexperienced to handle them. But how, as software engineers, should you go about establishing a more positive mindset?

It may be seen as common sense, but remember that your previous failures do not dictate your future successes. It is because of this that you need to remain engaged with the real world.

This means that social interaction is a must. Go for that coffee with a friend, call your son and daughter to do a puzzle with them, and play that video game that has been on your shelf for the past year. You need to make time for what causes you to be joyous, and if you are unable to do that, your quality of code will begin to deteriorate.

Software engineers are innovative by nature, thriving in a world where constant brain stimulation is present. Try to find a project that you are passionate about, and devote some time to it. You want to serve something that is bigger than yourself. That something will give you a sense of purpose whilst allowing you to engage with like-minded individuals. Whether it be designing a new diagnostic application or establishing a new online shopping tool that recommends foods based on your previous purchases, find that passion and pursue it.

Scope creeping

As a software engineer, you have probably heard of the term "scope creeping". However, for those who have not, let's break the term down more simply. Typically, when you start a project, your customer will give you a scope. This scope refines all of the requirements for the project, essentially so that the customer can get exactly what they require [21].

However, scope creeping refers to a project that has additional requirements added as the lifespan of the project continues. What this means is that as the software engineer, you are doing more work for exactly the same pay.

Scope creeping needs to be avoided, and here is how you can do it:

- Focus on and identify the core outcomes that have been stipulated in the scope.

- Ask yourself, "Is what I am doing in-line with the scope that was provided to me?" with regards to any changes that are requested of you, if they do not correspond with the initial scope, politely inform the customer that these specific changes will constitute extra work.

- If the customer starts to request drastic changes to the currently completed work, have a meeting with them to redefine what the scope's intention was, as well as their reasoning for the points in the scope.

- If you are finding it difficult to communicate with your customer, refer the case to your superior. If you are self-employed, ask other software engineers about their opinions of the situation.

- It is in this case that a scope creeping could put some undue strain on your ability to code effectively. However, the key is in being able to notice it quickly and rectify it before it gets out of hand.

As in all workplaces, you may find that there are some co-workers with whom you just do not gel. They may have rejected your aid when asking them about scope creeping, or they might enjoy blaming their errors on you. This is normal in many workplaces. However, it is important that these instances not be taken personally. Not only can this cause a downward spiral of depression, but it could also come with self-hatred.

You may start to think back on how you handled interactions with them, as well as what you could have done differently. The fact remains that what has been done and said will remain that way. The past cannot be changed, and harbouring an emotional attachment toward what is termed "industry hate" will not advance your career.

How many individuals combat this is through using these individuals as inadvertent mentors. They rethink their thought processes in the situation and identify flaws within themselves, providing insights that can help them grow personally and professionally.

Harbouring any form of resentment to another is not healthy and should be dealt with as soon as possible. Whether "dealing" with it is via introspection or visiting a psychologist, you will only genuinely be able to move forward once your personal feelings and actions have been dealt with and understood.

The selflessness of a software engineer knows no bounds. Ultimately, it is because of this that mental fatigue becomes apparent. A software engineer who has mental fatigue will find it difficult to focus on a task. This will most likely occur if a person is taking on back-to-back projects without a break in between. Some other symptoms of mental fatigue that one may experience include:

- Not being able to understand the information that you are receiving from somebody. This is not because you are intellectually disinclined, but because your mind refuses to take information in.

- A difficulty remembering dates of events, even if they were made recently.

- Difficulty being able to focus and streamline your thought processes in order to construct plans that solve a problem.

Mental fatigue remains one of the main causes of burnout, even with early detection. The reason for the latter is that although individuals can identify it, they do not know how to resolve it. Seeing as mental fatigue is based on a depleted mental capacity, utilizing restorative experiences in order to fill your mental energy gauge is advised. For many, this could be taking a walk-in nature, sitting by a pond, viewing wildlife, or watching a sunset. For others, replenishing their mental energy is structured around investing time in their interests.

A good time period that is suggested for this restorative practice is 30 minutes each day for three days per week. Not only will your restorative activities provide you with a calm mind that enables relaxation, but they will also aid in forgetting about all that worries you. Furthermore, this will allow you to perform some introspection and reflect on any personal matters that are troubling you.

Handling imposter syndrome

Imposter syndrome can be difficult to acknowledge and even trickier to navigate. However, before we delve deeper into how it affects a software engineer, we first need to define it. Imposter syndrome is the internal belief that your skill sets are not as advanced as others believe them to be. It does not matter how many hours you have poured into studying different coding languages or how many projects you have worked on, self-doubt has a way to always creep into your conscience.

The best approach for preventing imposter syndrome is to identify any signs of it as quickly as possible. Typically, those who berate their own performances, sabotage their own success, and attribute any signs of success to any other factor that is not their current skill set are more prone to developing imposter syndrome.

To provide context, imagine a software engineer saying they can write the next ground-breaking mobile application in two hours. Naturally, one would believe that this is impossible. However, even if the software engineer were to fall short, having fixated their mind on the challenge and not being able to complete it, they would enter into a negative spiral of self-doubt.

How imposter syndrome presents within the context of a software engineer is via the term "luck". You believe that the reason your written code works is because of luck rather than based on the skill and talent you possess. The thought process defines you as incompetent, which is definitely not the case!

With that being said, there are a wide variety of different causes for imposter syndrome. Some have developed it because they come from a family where achievement meant everything—what they achieved defined who they were as a person. Although doubt may present itself concerning whether you have imposter syndrome or not, try honestly answering the following questions:

- When you find a small mistake in your coding, do you feel worthless and incapable?

- When someone compliments you on your work, do you attribute your work's success to luck or other external factors?

- Do you find yourself downplaying your own skill sets, even when you know that you are more skilled than others?

If you do find you have developed imposter syndrome and are not able to acknowledge the hard work, sleepless nights, and hours of studying that you undertook to become a successful software engineer, we challenge you to think introspectively. Stop comparing your actions and results to those of others, especially when you use social media.

By assessing your abilities, you will be able to remain confident in what you know you are capable of doing [22]. If you feel you are not capable, then talk to someone about it. You do not want these irrational beliefs to well up and fester into untrue cognitive processes. You worked hard to get to where you are today, and you deserve to be acknowledged accordingly!

Companies you want to work for

A want to change, especially as a software engineer, cannot be overlooked. This change typically comes by looking for a new software company that provides more opportunities than your current one. However, you'll want to make sure that your next venture is a good fit for your career and that it offers opportunities for personal growth. Luckily, there are a few aspects that you can consider to make sure that you are a good fit for a prospective company and vice versa.

Large corporations, especially those that are well-known, will most likely have a rather high bar of entry. Seeing as so many individuals apply for these positions, you need to make sure your skills are on par with the best of the best. These companies provide interviews that are more practical than theoretical, focusing mostly on execution and quality. It is not uncommon for the interviewer to give you a scenario and ask you to create a code to solve that problem.

You will want to be able to grow in your trade, so you do not want to move into an organization where your theoretical knowledge is not challenged. You want to make sure that your company of choice is large enough to have automated a large deal of their digital processes. The reason you look for this is that instead of performing a repetitive action that could be automated, you will be focused on solving technical problems that will challenge you, evolving your skill sets and expertise.

A great software company will have a clear testing strategy. What this means is that they have a sufficient market share, product-market-fit, and understanding of customer needs. You want to work for a company that has a vision but that isn't distracted with the new before fixing all the potholes of the current. You will find that if you work with a company that remains transfixed with providing the customer with new features without any researched value, you will become demotivated and mentally exhausted in a matter of months [22].

As a software engineer, you need to ensure that your skills are up-to-date. Whether it be attending the latest coding and dev conference, or picking up an online course on a new coding language, you should look for a software company that is willing to aid you in achieving new heights. A company that will invest time and money into your personal and professional growth is one that understands your worth to them and the benefits your growth will bring them.

It is in this same light that you want to ensure that your workplace is well-equipped to perform the tasks required of you. Stay clear of companies that require you to purchase your own equipment to do their work. You want to go to a company where there is no need to worry about the functionality of tools that are present. For example, you do not want to worry about your 2005 laptop crashing while you are writing a large amount of code. The degree of stress that this imparts, if experienced over a long period of time, will become detrimental.

Taking all of the above into consideration, along with choosing a company that has a growing customer base, you should certainly be able to find a workplace that you feel comfortable in. As you start to interact with new customers, they will bring fresh perspectives and tasks that will alter your way of thinking. It is when you find a company that promotes these thought-provoking opportunities that not only is your growth guaranteed, but you will also find yourself happier when you wake up for work.

Working remote vs. office

With the adoption of working remotely, especially since the COVID-19 pandemic, many companies have shifted toward an online-only approach. It is this forced adaptation that has led to many aspects of an office job, such as attending meetings, to be shifted to an online medium.

As humans, we need social interaction, an aspect that has been lacking within our modern-day context. Moving everything online further decreases the amount of social interaction that we receive. It is this shift from in-person work to a remote style of work that has resulted in an altered lifestyle for employees (especially software engineers). However, the degree of this change will differ from person to person.

Working remotely does not mean that you are isolated and on your own. This is a misnomer that needs to be rectified. Working remotely can include sitting at an open-office co-working space where others are working but not necessarily for the same company.

Some individuals find these types of environments motivating, as everyone around you is working. However, others may find these same areas distracting, especially if the other individuals are talking loudly, making disrespectful levels of noise, and not being cognizant of those in their immediate space.

This is where the benefit of an office comes into play. Being able to close your door and isolate yourself from the immediate environment of noise and constant movement may be a motivating factor to some but a deterrent for others.

Studies are currently being conducted regarding the efficacy of working remotely in comparison to a typical office cubicle. Many different spheres are being tackled with this research, focusing on the levels of employee satisfaction achieved to that of the degree that noise affects one's arithmetic ability.

Within the software engineering field, some promising data has emerged. The results obtained by a study conducted by Georgia Tech shows that across 10,000 software development sessions, engineers would take 10 to 15 minutes after an interruption to get back into their flow of coding. This further makes one realize that a choice of working environment is a personalized decision. What works for some may not necessarily work for others.

One of the main points that have been brought up is the time that is saved when commuting. For those who use public transport, although they may save up to two hours a day if working remotely, many do utilize their commuting time effectively.

According to the Reuters Institute, 26% of all public commuters listen to podcasts during their commute. Even those who utilize their own means of transportation listen to podcasts as they commute (the same study showed this value to be 20% of all those that use their own transport). For many, a morning and evening commute provides their day with structure, which is automatically lost when working remotely provides them with free reign regarding how their day is organized.

There is no one-size-fits-all approach when deciding whether working remotely is preferred over an office cubicle. However, what we do know is that it does not matter whether you choose to work remotely or not; productivity remains one of the core outcomes that your company will expect from you. This is why you should put time and effort into finding an environment that works best for your needs and mental health [23].

Avoid the black hole of technical debt

Technical debt can be seen as a rather advanced term, especially when you are just starting out as a software engineer. However, putting it simply, it refers to the degree of liability that you or your company will incur due to code quality that is poor and sub-optimal. You can relate this to a diet program that you have heard will work with 100% of customers. Your intentions were good, but because the diet is not tailored specifically to you, your chance of successfully completing the diet decreases significantly.

Frustration is a key outcome of technical debt and tends to be a continuous downward spiral. As a software engineer, it is important that you tackle one problem at a time, completing each at once before tackling the next. As soon as you start to take on too many issues at a time, you become overwhelmed, ultimately finding yourself stuck in the black hole of technical debt. It is in this hole that your frustration and anxiety levels heighten, you will have trouble focusing, the code that you write is not yielding results, and your thought patterns are not linear.

The effects that the above have on your business prospects are severe. You may find that your technical debt causes limited (if any) scalability of your company's product and even a poor user experience augmented with high maintenance and operational costs. Falling into this hole of technical debt will create a void of disappointment and failure, which needs to be rectified immediately.

As a software engineer, experience will result in a decreased chance of falling into the black hole of technical debt. However, what can you do to eliminate the chance of technical debt occurring? You want to ensure that the architecture of your code is one that is flexible. For example, you would rather utilize a container-based architecture over one that requires refactoring. The reason for this is that the latter is not as sustainable when your skill sets are not extremely well-developed, along with the fact that changes that may need to be made are very costly.

Ensure that your code is routinely reviewed. When you constantly review your code, you are identifying immediate errors that could cause larger problems the further you code without rectifying it. This will enhance the quality of your code and reduce the chances and degree of technical debt occurring.

If you find yourself working on a rather large project as a lone ranger, automating your testing procedures will dramatically reduce the appearance of technical debt. Not only will automate testing save time for you to focus on more coding, but it also uncovers issues with a larger degree of precision in comparison to manual code testing.

Recording the changes that you make to the code, particularly when the code is being tested and edited by more than one person, is of great importance. It is as easy as placing the changes in an online repository that is accessible by the entire team. The main use of this is to track where the problems stem from and who made them, as well as to identify common errors that need to be promptly addressed.

Although the black hole of technical debt can be a daunting thought, there are many ways to circumvent any possibility of it occurring. As a software engineer, your main aim is to create quality code with minimal errors. In essence, you are a problem-solver. Preventing technical debt is no different and is easier to pre-empt than you think.

Chapter 12: Software Development Industry Secrets

*"It always takes longer than you expect, even when you take into account **Hofstadter's Law**"* -
Hofstadter's Law

Like any industry, there are industry secrets that one only becomes aware of, after working within the industry for a period of time. Some of these secrets are positive while others are negative, but by understanding them it may help to better prepare yourself for when you start working as a software engineer. Typically, insider secrets are not spoken about amongst individuals working in the industry for fear of reprisal. From my experience working as a software engineer below are some of the most common industry secrets.

Everyone sucks at the start

There are a number of software engineers who have experienced *'imposter syndrome'* which is essentially fearing that one does not possess the ability to complete a given task. As you start working as a software engineer you may feel other software engineers process information and develop software better than you.

Comparing yourself to others will likely add to the feeling of 'imposter syndrome'. But the truth is, the other software engineers are actually much better at developing software than you, mostly because they have x number of years more experience.

To get over imposter syndrome it's helpful to remember that almost everyone sucks at coding in the beginning. It's only by putting oneself into a lot of situations where you do not know the answer but refusing to quit until you get the answer does one start to become proficient at developing software.

Knowledge gaps

Software development is a big industry that encompasses a vast amount of knowledge. For this reason, it is impossible for anyone to have memorized (every concept, methodology or syntax.

Even within a single software language, it is difficult for a single person to remember all the syntax and best practices. This is why within the software engineer community it is recommended to learn concepts rather than specific programming syntax as syntax is always evolving and can be googled.

Google is your friend

Ex-Google, ex-Facebook software engineer and currently head of research at Comma.ai, **Geogre Hotz**, mentioned on a popular podcast, his reply to whenever he is asked a question, is to ask them to type the question into google because the top voted answer will provide a better answer than he ever could. Similarly, I have found that most of the major functionality or code that I have needed is just a google search away.

One of the biggest secrets in software development is a large proportion of code that is written nowadays, is actually derived from a google result. This is because most of the code that a software engineer would need, has already been written, tested and proofread by other software engineers on sites like **Stackoverflow** (one of the largest communities for software engineers to share their programming knowledge).

For this reason, finding code on credible forums is a more efficient way to build software than to write it yourself. However, even when you have the code for a specific functionality, you still need to edit it to suit your needs and fit it into your existing codebase.

Give credit

Developing software is a team sport, for this reason it's common for software engineers to help each other complete their respective tasks. Typically, this involves senior engineers providing a mentoring type role to the junior engineers. For this reason, it's useful to be cordial to the person who helps you. One way to stay cordial, is to always give them credit for when they have helped you.

Giving credit to the helper is best done in front of others such as, at the stand-up meeting where software engineers report to a manager listing the tasks they worked and will work on. By mentioning that the other person has helped you, during the stand-up meeting, you praise them in front of the manager and also demonstrate your soft skills.

From my own personal experience, I have found not giving credit to the helper reduces the chances they will help you again. So, it's also in a software engineers best interest to get into the habit of giving credit to the person who helped them.

Mental health

Software engineers have a higher chance of experiencing fatigue, burnout, anxiety and stress compared to workers who perform mechanical tasks [24]. Some argue this is due to the 'start up culture' which encourages engineers to work eighty-hour weeks and software development being an industry which attracts introverted depressive types.

In any case, I have found it useful to ensure my mental health is a priority over any software development work by not working overtime, managing expectations and having hobbies which do not require the use of a computer.

Side projects

Side projects will make you a better engineer and might even get you some exciting opportunities. A software development project that you work on outside of your normal job is considered a side project. However, in this chapter, "side projects" means a project that could provide value and could result in monetary income.

Side projects provide a security blanket in case your current job decides to let you go. They do this by first demonstrating your coding abilities as well as providing monetary income. There are numerous side projects one could work on, which could include building web and mobile applications, contributing to open source software or building websites. As you can imagine, employers would be very impressed to see that you already have software that is available to the public.

Managing expectations

Managing expectations in software means communicating to the project manager what to expect and when to expect it by. Early in my career as a software engineer, I was eager to impress. This sometimes resulted in overpromising and under delivering which I believe contributed to me eventually burning out.

The hard part for a software engineer is accurately predicting what task is possible and how long it will take. This difficulty is expressed in **Hofstadter's Law** which is used to describe the difficulty in estimating the time it will take to complete a task of substantial complexity. Below is listed some tips to avoid giving inaccurate estimates for a task or project.

- Do not give an estimate until you fully understand what is required.
- Factor in time for bugs, testing, pull requests and other miscellaneous tasks.
- Have a high-level understanding of where the feature would fit in the code base.
- Give estimates with a confidence range i.e. "60% confident it will take two weeks".

Although one may have the best intentions when giving a kind estimate, it does not help you or your manager. When giving an estimate of how long a task will take, I have found it's best to under promise and over deliver.

Workplace politics

Workplace politics is where individuals use power and social networking to achieve their aims. There are positive political behaviours in the workplace that benefit the company and individuals such as publicizing one's accomplishments or praising others. On the other hand, there are negative political behaviours which are meant to achieve personal gain at the expense of others. For example, spreading rumours, talking behind someone's back or purposefully withholding information.

Software development is not exempt from negative political behaviours in the workplace. One-way software engineers may do this, is through, 'knowledge hiding'. Which is purposefully withholding information from others in order to maintain their reputation for knowing 'unique information'. Knowledge hiding behaviours include providing inaccurate information, pretending not to know what others are talking about or using bullying tactics to make the other person feel guilty for asking questions.

It is useful to be aware of these negative political behaviours in the workplace. Because when they appear, you are able to recognise and act accordingly. Not recognizing these behaviours can sometimes lead to being unhappy, stress and eventually burnout.

Writing documentation

Writing documentation in software development means writing short concise explanations of code that has been written. In software engineer communities, it is often said 'Good code doesn't need documentation'. One of the features of good code is that it "reads like a story". This means there is a naming convention that accurately describes each part of the code, so that the reader knows the functionality that each part belongs to.

With increasing demands of users, software can become very complex and it can unclear how different sections of the code are linked. Also, with public APIs becoming the norm for software companies, writing documentation to explain the APIs usage is essential. For this reason, software engineers are sometimes expected to write documentation about the software they have written.

Always be learning

Computer programming is a vast field and is beyond a single person's ability to fully understand. Because it's such a large field, you never have to stop learning. And if you do decide to stop learning, whether you're a software engineer lead or a junior engineer I would strongly recommend against that. This is because as frameworks and languages constantly change, learning them will become essential to having a long career in software development.

Chapter 13: Advice to future software engineers

"Always code as if the guy who ends up maintaining your code will be a violent psychopath who knows where you live" - Rich Osborne

Marathon not a sprint

If you have invested your time in reading this book, it is likely you are a highly motivated individual, who is eager to get a job as a software engineer. Whilst being highly motivated is helpful, I would suggest keeping in mind that becoming a software engineer is a long-term goal, and is achieved by learning in small increments, ideally through daily practice.

I like to think of studying software development (in fact any complex subject) as a thousand-piece jigsaw puzzle and each day you fit two pieces together, and after some time the jigsaw is complete.

By having this long-term perspective, you prevent trying to learn everything in a short period of time which reduces the retaining information you are trying to learn and can even lead to burn out. In fact, maintaining the mindset of doing things in small increments is useful anytime you build software.

By building software in incremental stages, you allow yourself to sit back and hone in on each incremental piece of software which will reduce technical debt, reduce chance of burnout and make the process of building software more enjoyable.

Fall in love with coding

Like any other career, if you enjoy what you do you will never have to work a day in your life. Being a software engineer is one of the few careers where you can fall in love with your craft. The below quote by Sandi Metz in her book **Object Oriented-Design in Ruby** succinctly summarises what it is, to craft software:

"Those of us whose work is to write software are incredibly lucky. Building software is a guiltless

pleasure because we get to use our creative energy to get things done. We have arranged our lives to have it both ways; we can enjoy the pure act of writing code in sure knowledge that the code we write has use.

We produce things that matter. We are modern craftspeople, building structures that make up present day reality, and no less than bricklayers or bridge builders, we take justifiable pride in our accomplishments. This all programmers share, from the most enthusiastic newbie to the apparently jaded elder, whether working at the lightest weight Internet start-up or the most staid, long-entrenched enterprise. We want to do our best work. We want our work to have meaning. We want to have fun along the way." - Sandi Metz

Levelling up

In order to improve your skills as a software engineer it is vital that you practice. This can mean learning theory, practice solving algorithms, coding applications, testing, debugging and building projects. Whatever you are practicing it is wise to do it often, in order to maintain the habit.

As mentioned previously, setting daily goals to achieve proficiency in coding is required to become proficient. I personally experienced optimal results when I practiced coding for two to three hours per day. By practicing irregularly, progress will be limited. With learning any complex skill, developing a habit of practice and staying disciplined is useful for long term progress and by practicing every day, your skills compound over time.

Document your journey

Documenting your journey to become a software engineer through a blog, YouTube or another social media avenue is a great way to market yourself in today's competitive job market. Employers often research an applicant's online presence, and by having a coding orientated online presence, it demonstrates your passion and motivation for software, which may put you ahead of applicants who do not have an online presence. Furthermore, it can provide additional opportunities such as additional income streams, networking and job opportunities.

Documenting your journey could mean a blog or video outlining what you've been learning and the roadblocks you have faced in the past week. Some individuals may not feel comfortable sharing what they have been working on and could choose to create coding tutorials demonstrating their ability.

I've personally documented my journey by creating coding tutorials on YouTube, which has provided job opportunities and additional income streams. Whilst there are many positives to having an online presence, some larger companies believe it is a risk because you may share sensitive information.

Saving and investing

When starting any career, it's useful to think further down the road. This is especially the case in software development, where the majority of software engineers quit after working 15 years in the industry [25]. Because the typical career length is so short for software engineers, it's useful to start saving and investing the money you earn into a nest egg that can provide you with income further down the road.

There is a lot of debate regarding the most profitable place to invest, some argue that real estate has the highest returns where as others are in favour of investing in the stock market. This book does not have an answer on the best place to invest, but the key message of this section is to save and invest in an asset that has a high probability of returning income that can offer monetary security.

One of the main reasons for investing, is the income you receive from your job is not guaranteed. At any moment, you could be let go. And as a software engineer gets older, it becomes harder to land software engineering jobs, as the job market tends to favour younger applicants.

Ideally you should calculate your total expenditure per month and aim to make investments that return the total expenditure amount. By having investments that return your expenditure amount, you create a safety net in case you are let go from your job.

Mentorship

Mentorship is where a more experienced person helps to guide a less experienced person. This can be extremely helpful when you reach a sticking point while learning, or even if you have personal issues. Mentors can also provide much needed reassurance and guidance whilst applying for jobs. Moreover, by having a mentor, you can get an idea of what a high level of coding proficiency looks like (provided you have a good mentor).

In a software company, it is common for senior engineers to mentor the junior engineers. However, when you do not have a job, finding a mentor can be difficult. You may wish to visit your local coding communities, or use a service like **Code Mentor**.

Conclusion

In summary, working as a software engineer can be a rewarding job; financially and spiritually. However, it can come with negatives, for example; risk of overworking. On my own journey I experienced both the negative and positive aspects, but for me the positives far outweigh the negatives.

If, after extensive research you have decided working in software is what you would like to do, the first and most important step you can take, is to discipline yourself to study daily for a sustained period of time. In my experience, most individuals are not doing this, which is the reason for their lack of progress. I do hope you can be one of the few who do study and code on a consistent basis.

Many thanks for taking the time to read this book. I sincerely hope that this book helps you land your first software engineering job. If you need to reach out to me feel free to contact me via the contact form on my website **https://hasanarmstrong.com/**. If you have enjoyed this book, it would mean a lot to me, if you could leave a review.

I've also included a bonus CV template that myself and others have used to apply for a software engineer role, which you can access by emailing me at **hasan_armstrong@hotmail.co.uk**.

THE END

References

[1] Figure 12 of Hauser, Robert M. 2002. "Meritocracy, cognitive ability, and the sources of occupational success." Available at **https://www.iqcomparisonsite.com/Occupations.aspx**

[2] *Bulletin of the World Health Organization* 2019;97:585-586. Doi. Available at **https://www.who.int/bulletin/volumes/97/9/19-020919/en/**

[3] Blue light from light-emitting diodes elicits a dose-dependent suppression of melatonin in humans. Available at **https://pubmed.ncbi.nlm.nih.gov/21164152/**

[4] The Brugger Relief Position for Posture Correction. Available at: **https://www.youtube.com/watch?v=-4r1tgG6ZCM**

[5] Social Isolation and Memory Decline in Later-life. Available at: **https://academic.oup.com/psychsocgerontology/article/75/2/367/5645554**

[6] Stuck on a Problem? Why You Should Take a Break. Available at: **https://www.success.com/stuck-on-a-problem-take-a-break/**

[7] 3m Visual Attention Service. Available at: **https://multimedia.3m.com/mws/media/1006827O/3msm-visual-attention-software-vas-validation-study.pdf**

[8] Most coders have sleep problems. Available at: **https://www.theregister.com/2010/11/23/coders_insomnia_mental_hygiene/**

[9] 10 Tips to Improve your Communication Skills as a Software Developer. Available at: **https://www.codingame.com/blog/10-tips-to-improve-your-communication-skills-as-a-software-developer/**

[10] Anki. Available at: **https://apps.ankiweb.net/**

[11] Deep work: Rules for Focused Success in a Distracted World. Available at: **https://www.amazon.co.uk/Deep-Work-Focused-Success-Distracted/dp/0349411905**

[12] Kanban Flow. Available at: **https://kanbanflow.com/**

[13] A time to think: circadian rhythms in human cognition. Available at: **https://pubmed.ncbi.nlm.nih.gov/18066734/**

[14] Dress for success how clothes influence our performance. Available at: **https://www.psychologicalscience.org/news/ dress-for-success-how-clothes-influence- our-performance.html**

[15] Here is the time in the day when you're most productive. Available at: **https://www.psychologytoday.com/us/blog/ why-bad-looks-good/201808/here-is-the- time-day-when-you-are-most-productive**

[16] Agile vs Waterfall: A Comparative analysis. Available at: **http://ijsetr.org/wp- content/uploads/2014/10/IJSETR-VOL-3- ISSUE-10-2680-2686.pdf**

[17] Podcasts: Who, Why, What, and Where? Available at: **https://www.digitalnewsreport.org/survey/2 019/podcasts-who-why-what-and-where/**

[18] How to network as a software developer. Available at: **https://learnitmyway.medium.com/how-to-network-as-a-software-developer-2bab6cba09fc**

[19] Side Gigs That Will Make You Money as a Programmer in 2020. Available at: **https://medium.com/better-programming/side-gigs-that-will-make-you-money-as-a-programmer-in-2020-9124760f3c8**

[20] Is there a software developer age limit? Available at: **https://searchsoftwarequality.techtarget.com/opinion/Is-there-a-software-developer-age-limit-Apparently-its-45**

[21] What is Scope Creep in Project Management? Available at:

https://www.wrike.com/project-management-guide/faq/what-is-scope-creep-in-project-management/

[22] Signs of a Great Software Engineering Organization. Available at: https://www.byteperceptions.com/career-management/signs-of-a-great-software-engineering-organization.html

[23] 31 Tips to Boost Your Mental Health | Mental Health America. https://www.mhanational.org/31-tips-boost-your-mental-health

[24] Anxiety and Mental Health of Software Professionals and Mechanical Professionals. Available at: http://www.ijhssi.org/papers/v3(2)/Version-2/G0322052056.pdf

[25] Programmers: Before you turn 40, have a plan B. Available at: **https://improvingsoftware.com/2009/05/19/ programmers-before-you-turn-40-get-a-plan-b/**